LIBRARY AND INFORMATION SCIENCE
CONCEPTS, PRACTICES & SERVICES

LIBRARY AND INFORMATION SCIENCE

CONCEPTS, PRACTICES & SERVICES

SHABIR AHMAD
BILAL AHMAD DAR

Ess Ess Publications
New Delhi

LIBRARY AND INFORMATION SCIENCE
CONCEPTS, PRACTICES & SERVICES

ISBN : 978-93-87698-27-7

First Published 2019

Published by:
Ess Ess Publications
4831/24, Ansari Road,
Darya Ganj,
New Delhi-110 002.
INDIA
Phones: 23260807, 41563444
Fax: 41563334
E-mail: info@essessreference.com
www.essessreference.com

Cover Design by *Patch Creative Unit*

Printed and bound in India

Dedicated to

My Parents And My Teacher,

Mentor And Guide

DR. KHAISAR MUNEEBULLA KHAN

Contents

Preface

Library has always been the main instrument for the socio-economic, cultural and intellectual development of any society. As a service oriented organization, libraries acquire, organize and facilitate the use of information and knowledge for the welfare of an individual and the society at large. Without timely and expeditious use and utilization of information, every facet of human existence will be halted since the information rules the roost in our times. It would not be wrong to say that the modern society is truly and rightly known as Information Society, a society where in every aspect of the human endeavour is information and knowledge driven and the main objective of the library professional is to provide the right information to the right user at the right time. This is why, in the changing environment, the role of a library has changed from document management to knowledge management. A modern society requires a modern library with highly skilled library professionals to maximize the utilization of services and products of libraries so as to reach out to their clients and fulfil their information needs. As reflected, Libraries are the path breakers, but the paths they break will be characterized more by their divergence than their similarity, which can be achieved by assimilating the fundamental concepts of librarianship. Under the backdrop of information superhighway, revolutionized by information communication technologies (ICTs), computers, internet, social media, RFIDs, cloud computing, networking, consortia, big data, digital media coupled with boom of digital information, E-Resources and other concepts, writing a monograph on basic fundamentals, concepts and Practices of librarianship may be questioned by some professionals. But, if there has been any need and relevance for such a monograph to acquaint budding professionals and students of LIS, then it is in this very age of information explosion. To be well versed and acquainted with the fundamental concepts of librarianship is as important as keeping abreast with the latest and emerging concepts of LIS profession for any working professional, student, teacher or researcher. In the age ICT era, Libraries and LIS education has given rise to revolutionary changes, publishing being one of them, as it has supplemented it rather than making it irrelevant as some would argue.

The present book introduces a professional to a plethora of concepts, practices, issues and challenges from basic concept of librarianship to its advanced allied services. The chapters have been designed to give a clear and comprehensive insight into the intriguing concepts and topics. The concepts, topics and practices in the book have been dealt with simplicity yet explicitly. The chapterization of the book is as following: 1. Library, Information and Society, 2. Public Library System in India, 3.

Information Resources and Services, 4. Impact of Information Technology on Library & Information Education and Trainings and 5. Recent Trends in Library and Information Science Education In India and Aboard. Thus the book is a blend of basic and fundamental principles of LIS to modern and innovative emerging concepts, issues and strategies of LIS education. The authors have made every effort to include major concepts, ideas, practices and relevance to a working professional, students of LIS, research scholars or an academician, but still lacunas in terms of its coverage and selection of topics might have remained. Suggestions and professional advice from the readers are welcome for improving the quality and spectrum of this book and will be incorporated in the revised editions which hopefully will follow in future.

— Authors

1

Library, Information And Society

1.1. INTRODUCTION

The libraries are the main element for the development of a modern society. As service agencies, they organize and facilitate the use of information and knowledge for the development of an individual as well as the society. It is in this broad perspective, the main motive and objective of the Library and information profession is to provide the right information to the right user at the right time with a right attitude. Libraries and library services are absolutely essential to achieve the developmental goals, improve the quality of life and preserve and make known the country's as well as the states cultural heritage in its multiple formats. In other words libraries serve as intellectual catalyst for socio-economic development by providing facilities of the purpose of acquiring Education, information, recreation, aesthetic appreciation and research.

In Modern societies, every human activity is organized through institutions. Every major social task, whether economic performance or health care, Education or research, business or industry is institutionalized. Libraries and other similar types of institutions are those that collect, stock, process organize, disseminate and distribute information and knowledge recorded in the documents. Since, knowledge and information are so vital for all round human development, Libraries and Information institutions that are entrusted with the task of information collection, organization and dissemination are indeed invaluable. Thus, unlike the other institutions each of which concentrates on one or a few of the needs of society, the library is able to serve almost all its needs. The libraries provide a world of different experience – books that will give you knowledge, bring to surface your latent aesthetic talents, stimulate your intellect, inculcate values and learning skills in you, provide you with recreation and exposes you with your cultural heritage and traditions. Therefore, of all the institutions founded by society, the library and its modern cognates that are the most potent and promising in meeting the multifarious of different users of modern society. Libraries and society are related with each other from hundreds of years in serving diverse communities.

Libraries play a fundamental role in society. Libraries, through the documents, are actually Repositories of information and knowledge and play a fundamental role in the society. They have been acting like gateways to Knowledge and culture, learning resources and services which further create opportunities for learning, support literacy and education. They have myriad ways to shape the new ideas and perspectives that are central to a creative and innovative society. The basic information role of the library is to collect material containing information through appropriate methods. It is primarily in this sense that a library is described as an information Centre. They have been responsible ensuring an aesthetic record of knowledge created and accumulated by past generations. Libraries have been an agent to advance research and human knowledge or preserve the world's cumulative knowledge and heritage.

1.1.1. Meaning and Definition of a Library

Library is a place where information resources are organized for use. A library refers to a place where literary and artistic materials are kept for the purpose of reading and research. Etymologically, the word "library" is derived from the Latin word 'libraria 'meaning 'a book place'. It originates from the term "liber" which means "a book". In English, the word library means "a collection of books for study, Research, reference and recreation. The definition and meaning library has changed drastically over a period of time with the change in its use and function. In the past a library was considered "a place where books were written or kept". This term was frequently used as a "collection of books" and a Librarian was considered and assigned duties as a keeper or guard of books. Earlier, library was considered a storehouse of books. The main function of a library was to preserve human thought and knowledge of the society. But, the developments and transformation that have taken place during the last two centuries have transformed the libraries and Functions and the services have changed also. The entire outlook of libraries has been changed due to the way it started offering its services in the society and the way people expect it to function. Let's analyze some definitions provided by different reference sources and the scholars of library and information science.

The oxford English Dictionary (OED) defines library as, "a building or room containing collections of books, periodicals and sometimes films and recorded music for using or borrowing by the public or the members of an institution." The Merriam Webster's Dictionary defines it as, "a place in which literary, musical, artistic, or reference materials (as books, manuscripts, recordings, or films) are kept for use but not for sale."

The Oxford Companion to the English Language says that the 'Library is a collection of books, periodicals and/or other materials, primarily written and printed.' The Harold's librarian's Glossary and Reference Book explains library as.

I. A collection of books and other literary material kept for reading studying and consultation.

II. A place, building room or rooms set apart for keeping the books.

III. A collection of films, photographs and other non-books materials, plastic or metal tapes, disks, and programs.

From the above delimitations it can be easily deduced that a library is essentially "A physical space such as a building, part of a building, rooms or room or such a place having collections or collection of intellectual or literary output of a society such as manuscripts, books periodicals, newspapers, pamphlets, written or printed records, tape, artifacts or any literary and artistic materials for reading, reference, or lending purpose."

Lastly, it will be very prudent to provide the view point of S.R. Ranganathan about the library. He says 'a library is a public institution or establishment charged with the care of collection of books and the duty of making then accessible to those who require to use them."

1.1.2. Purpose of a Library:

Library has been given the states of a public institution. Being a public institution, a library spells out its goals and objectives and has the responsibility to serve the public without any reservation or biasness. It shoulders the purpose of organization, maintenance and preservation of aspects of the library collections, so that it can serve the society or a community for a longer period. The ultimate purpose of a library is the make library holdings/ materials available to the public for use or consultation. Hence, the purpose of a library is to serve the society through the records of human thoughts, ideas, and expressions by making them available as an when required by the members of the society, and preserving them for the coming generations, as these records are the intellectual wealth of the society. It plays an important role in supporting the educational and research activities of society, promoting culture, disseminating information, catering to the spiritual and ideological instincts in man and building up a value system for him and providing recreation.

1.1.3. Functions of a library

As the society developed and progressed, the responsibilities and functions of a library also increased. The major two indispensable functions of a library in the modern society are preservation of the intellectual heritage of the society in the form of literary works known as information sources and making these information sources accessible to the people of the society. The functions of a library can be studied under following major headings system:

(a) Education : Libraries are the backbone of any Education system. Libraries provide means for self-development of the individuals and masses at various stages of education. The libraries close the gap between an individual and recorded knowledge. Being the Centre of any educational setup, the libraries support and promote all types of education, be it formal, no-formal or adult and life-long. This is achieved by the acquiring and organizing of documents for the community. Basically, the special function of the public library to work for the education of the illiterate people in its community through audio-visual media. Library also support the education of working groups by enhancing their vocations and physically handicapped are now-a-days served through audio-visual media.

(b) Information Dissemination : Libraries, through their information resources, are actually repositories of information and knowledge. Information is indispensable for any human activity aiming at social progress. Libraries help to provide accurate and current information to individuals and masses. The scope of information service is extended to included information on socio-economic needs of the society. A library serves as information dissemination. Information about every aspect of the human activity is collected, organized an ultimately disseminated to the general public.

(c) Promotion of Culture : The primary function of a library is that it preserves the cultural heritage of the human race as represented by the books and other documents it possess. It supports cultural activities by making books available which would bring to expression the creative talents of individuals and develop their faculties for aesthetic appreciation. It also organize cultural Programs like music concerts, Dances, Dramas, Painting competitions for children exhibitions of rare book collections and cultural of gatherings, seminars, symposia, paintings and thus enrich the cultural life of the community. Thus, libraries function as the principal centers of cultural life and promote culture at various levels. Promotion of culture has two aspects, firstly, reading and thinking, that widens mental horizon and develops creative capabilities of the individuals. Secondly, the library has to contribute to the cultural enrichment of the society.

(d) Recreation and Leisure : The healthy use of leisure is a matter of great importance in community life so that leisure time is not developed to negative and destruction activities. The library caters to the recreational and leisure needs of its users by providing information sources for the purpose. Novels and other forms of literature, works of art, books of travels, biographies, popular magazines etc are primarily books of recreation and find place in every library. Thus, provision of scope for healthy or positive use of leisure time is an important function of a library. Audio-Visual materials such as films, TV, Radios, audio-video cassettes etc are heavenly provided for recreation purposes.

(e) Spiritual and Religion : Libraries have also an important function of spiritual and religious upliftment of the society. Spiritual and religious books, books that have profound ideological themes and other books of permanent Value which may be described as classes are books of inspiration. They meet the spiritual, religious and ideological needs of their readers. In short, the functions of libraries can be summed up as:

i. Foster, and promote the spread of knowledge, education.

ii. Provide facility for formal and non-formal life/culture long self-education in the community.

iii. Preserve the literary and cultural heritage of humanity for posterity as vehicles of culture and material for research,

iv. Provide reliable information for all kinds of users irrespective of age, caste, creed, colour, religion, sex etc.

v. Collect resources in order to promote an enlightened citizenship and to enrich personal life.

vi. Facilitate advancement of culture in the community.

vii. Collect, maintain and make the information sources available to the people of a society to help them to make themselves aware of the available literates.

1.2. ROLE OF LIBRARY IN SOCIETY

Modern Society cannot think of without a robust and balanced library system. Libraries are indispensable for the progress and development of a society. Libraries play a important role in the Socio-economic, cultural and educational development of society. Over the centuries, libraries have developed different models to serve the society. Presently, we have different types of libraries to cater the wide range of informational needs of the society. Broadly, there are three models of libraries namely,

A. Academic libraries.

B. Public libraries

C. Special libraries and

D. One Unique model- National Library

which together play a vital role in socio-economic political and cultural development of a community and society. Let us study some main roles of libraries.

1.2.1. Role of libraries in Education

Education and training of the individual is considered on essential means of stimulating economic and social development libraries and educational institutions are two faces of the same coin, one cannot survive without the other. The purpose of the education cannot be fulfilled without a library. Library is often called a hub of educational activities and heart of educational institutions with which it is attached. To make the people erudite and civilized the society requires an effective educational system which is itself impossible without a good library system. Without libraries there can neither be any good school, college or university nor any life-long education of adults be encouraged. It is believed that where formal education ends, informal education begins and a life-long learning process is sustained with the support of adequate and proper library services. Libraries support the teaching and learning process at all levels of education. Library inculcates reading habits in students and provides knowledge in the subjects of pursuits. It helps in developing critical and analytical thinking, and develops habits of self-study of help in the intellectual development of a student.

2.2.2. Role of library in Research and Development

Supporting research is another role of the library. Access to existing knowledge and information is essential for research. The knowledge that is newly created is primarily communicated through journals, research reports and other similar publications. Every library attached to an institutions engaged in research should have a strong collection of such publications to support research programs. The human activities in the modern society are based on creating and utilizing information and further converting it into economic resources. Hence, the library provides support to the research and development work of a researcher as well as institutions. The libraries attached to universities, research institutions and organizations play the key role in this respect. Even public libraries have a research role especially in the social sciences and humanities.

1.2.3. Role of Library in Information Dissemination

Libraries, through their books, are actually repositories of information and knowledge. Information is indispensable for any human activity aiming at social progress. Every individual, researcher, teacher, student administrators, artisan, entrepreneur, farmer all need information and approach a library for satisfying their informational needs to equip themselves better for the fruitful pursuit of their respect vocations. For this purpose, the library collects the informational materials required by the various sections of the society. With the help of library services, the library disseminates the information among the individual of the society. Apart from this, the library organizes seminars, workshops, exhibitions and a lot of other programs which help people in acquiring knowledge and skills. With the help of formal and informal library services the library disseminates information in the society either through books, journals, periodicals etc. or by organizing programs with the help of experts of different field. It is primarily in this sense that a library is described as an information centre.

1.2.4. Role of library as social Institutions

Library services are considered as a social necessity for the steady development and progress of a person as a social being as well as of a society. As a social institution, it helps in life-long self education and furnishes up-to-date facts and information on all subjects. It provides opportunities for positive use of leisure time and preserves the literary and cultural heritage of humanity for posterity. It works for continued social well-being of the society, as an agency of change of all socialized recorded thoughts. Libraries enhance the level of intelligence and studies of the common man in the society to a great extent. The library tends to increase the reading habits and change the reading tastes of the people by raising their cultural level. A civilized society is expected to have literate an educated community fully aware of the value, importance and use of libraries. The library is, thus, a driving force capable of building a better society by its nature, variety quality and extent of service. Being a social institution, library not only satisfies the readers by providing books, but also promotes the desire for books. As a social institution, library allows its users to interact among themselves. A library provides a right forum for social get-together within its premises and makes it available an equal terms to all groups in the community. Libraries are the foundation in the endeavour of civic and social responsibilities and a positive role in the development of a society. It is under such an endeavour, libraries are essentially considered as "People University". Libraries have a very important role to play in the fields of political awareness, socio-economic growth, cultural and educational enlightment which are indispensable to the future development of any country. Libraries serve to all classes of people and acts as an intellectual catalyst by providing facilities for acquiring education, information recreation, aesthetic appreciation and research, irrespective of age and sex for the welfare of the society as a whole.

1.3. LIBRARY AND THE CHANGING SOCIETY

A society does not remain static but goes on changing. Library being a social institution also reflects the changes in its operations and work. The present day society has undergone transformation in almost all sectors. Library and society are inter-linked and inter-dependent. There is a strong perception that the development in a society is not possible without a library. The society we live in today has been termed as information society as maximum population is engaged in professions where information's and technologies are both raw as well as finished products of the human efforts. The present day society is the result of collective intellectual human endeavours for centuries. Several factors are responsible for this transformation. The main factors are:

- Pressures exerted by the population explosion, increasing urbanization group dynamics etc.
- Socio-economic changes affect occupational patterns, incomes, prices, value, inflation, and growth dynamics.
- Political changes which affect political structures and systems.
- Educational changes which affect learning and teaching process at all levels of education.
- Research and development in the scientific and technological fields, the social sciences and humanities.
- Trade and commerce, import and export, international trade and commerce, Globalization etc.
- High standard of living.
- Well established book trade.

- Multi-media and Mass Communication.
- Information communication Technology (ICT)

These social, political and economic conditions have left a great impact on all aspects of the growth of libraries, radically changing their conventional functions. Modern library not only deals with books but collects informationin a multi-media for its uses. The modern library has undergone tremendous changes in handling the basic functions and operations of a library viz, collection, processing, storage, retrieval, dissemination and utility of information. New information communication and networking technologies have completely changed the functioning of the libraries. Information is collected, processed, stored and disseminate using sophisticated technologies. The new demands of users have to be met by several activities based upon documentation, information analysis consolidation and repacking computer based information systems, many of these developments have also provided new opportunities for commercialization of information products and services, thus paving the way for information for an information industry which is growing and flourishing steadily. Although, the library essentially handles information and knowledge, the institutional mechanism to meet the demands of users in an information society has expanded by properly organizing and operating many of the modern information systems and services.

If we visualize the picture of development of a society, we find that the whole process has revolved around information and knowledge. Thus, libraries have become the backbone of the development process. With the various changes taking place in the society the role of library has also changed dynamically. The library in modern society is being considered a service Agency. It organizes and facilitates the use of information and knowledge for the development of an individual as well as the society.

1.4. TYPES OF LIBRARIES AND THEIR FUNCTIONS

In the previous discussions, we have discussed about the need, importance, functions and role of libraries in the society. It is now clear that libraries of all kinds play an important role in socio-economic, cultural and educational development of a society. The libraries strength literacy among the people, library services improve knowledge and skills of people for positive productivity thereby contributing to national development. The information needs of the society differ from community to community and institutions to institution. On the basis of varied informational needs of the society, different models of libraries have been developed. Broadly, libraries have been grouped into four categories on the basis of their objectives and functions in the society. The four categories of libraries are as under:

I. Public libraries.

II. Academic library <school> college> university.

III. Special libraries.

IV. National libraries.

1.4.1. Public library

Among the different types of libraries evolved by society in modern times, public libraries are the most popular because of the functions they perform. They play a very significant role in the welfare of the society. Public library is a social institution established for providing opportunities to each and every person of the society, irrespective of their cast, creed, religion, gender, social, economic and educational status, etc to acquire knowledge through reading materials. It is established for general public and is maintained chiefly by public fund. It is an integral part of the community it serves. Mankind has taken decades, rather centuries to evolve this institution. It would be worthwhile to know the factors which have helped in the evolution of a public library. These are:

- People urge for knowledge.
- Improvement of literacy level through self-education.
- Universal public education.
- As an information dissemination Centre.
- Enlightened leadership and philanthropy.
- Rapid Advancement in science Technology.
- To be community's intellectual Centre.
- Fruitful utilization of Leisure.

Meaning and Definition of public library

A public library is a non-profit library established for the use of the general public and maintained chiefly by public funds. In other words, a public library is for the public, by the public and of the public. Public library has been defined differently by different experts, depending upon the importance they gave to its objectives. It is a people University for those who laid stress on educative aspect; it was a common man's cultural centre for those who had in mind its recreational role; for some it was a centre to provide authentic information for various aspects of life. The public library research group of the united kingdom states that the basic aim of a public library is "to contribute to sustain the quality of life in all its aspects-educational economic, industrial, scientific and cultural and promote the concept of democratic society in which equal opportunity exists for all, to develop into true citizens, with whole and balanced personalities leading to an increase in the sum total of man's happiness and awareness of himself, his fellow men and his environment." Hence, we can say that the public library is a social institution with the responsibility of providing library services to the community, without any bias and prejudice to cater to its informational to each and every member of the society to achieve success in life which ultimately contributes to the development of the society. It provides service to every citizen irrespective of one's birth, caste, colour, sex, social, economic and educational standard without any cost.

UNESCO Public Library Manifesto

The UNESCO's public library manifesto was formulated for its member countries in 1949, to promote the public library system and make knowledge accessible to each and every member of the society. This Manifesto was further revised in 1972 and was again revised in 1994 in collaboration with International Federation of library Associates and Institutions (IFLA). The Manifesto provides guidelines regarding objectives, activities, and services of public library, and its funding, legislation and networks, its operations, management and implementation.

According to the manifesto, public library is the local gateway to knowledge. It provides basic conditions for lifelong learning, independent decision making and cultural development of an individual as well as social group. This manifesto proclaims the UNESCO's belief in the public library as a living force for education culture, and information and an essential agent for fostering peace and spiritual welfare in the society, through the minds of men and women. Also, manifesto ascertains it as a local centre of information, making all kinds of knowledge and information readily and freely available to its users. The public library should be accessible for all, regardless of age, race, sex relation, nationality, language or social status. And lastly, public library material must reflect current trends and the evolution of society, as well as the memory of human endeavour and imagination.

Key Missions of Public Library

The following are key missions of public libraries as provided by the UNESCO's public library manifesto which relate to information, literacy, education and culture and should be at the core of public library services.

- Creating and strengthening reading skills and habits

in children from an early age;

- Supporting both individual and self-conducted education as well as formal education;
- Providing opportunities for personal creative development;
- Stimulating the imagination and creativity of children and young people;
- Promoting awareness of cultural heritage; appreciation of the arts, scientific achievements and innovations;
- Providing access to cultural expressions of all performing;
- Fostering inter-cultural dialogue and favoring art; cultural diversity;
- Supporting the oral traditions;
- Ensuring access for citizens to all sorts of community information.
- Providing adequate information services to local enterprises, associations and interest groups;
- Facilitating the development of information and computer literacy skills,
- Supporting and participating in literacy activities and programs for all age groups, and initiating such activities, if necessary.

With these key missions, the public libraries will enable the development of well informed citizens capable of exercising their democratic rights and play responsive role in the changing society. This will generally depend in a free flow of unlimited access to public libraries. In short, the UNESCO's public library is expected to play its role mainly in three principal area viz, information, education and culture.

It has to serve as a:

- Centre for information.

- Centre for self-education.
- Centre for culture and
- Centre for local cultural materials
- Centre for development of democratic spirit.
- Centre for an impartial service agency.

Objectives of public library

Dr. S.R. Ranganathan in his Book "Library Manual", lays down the following objectives of the public library.

I. It should help the life-long self-education of one and all;

II. It should furnish up-to-date facts and information on all subjects to one and all;

III. It should distribute in an unbiased and balanced way, all recreated views and thoughts to one and all, as a help in discharge of their political functions in respect of local, national and international affairs.

IV. It should contribute to the productivity drive by informing top management of the latest trends in diverse enterprises, by ploughing back into the minds of researcher's designers, and technologists every piece of relevant new thought, promptly and pin-pointedly.

V. It should provide one and all a harmless and elevating use of leisure;

VI. It should preserve the literary remains of humanity for posterity as vehicles of culture and as source materials for antiquarian research;

VII. In general, it should work for continued social well-being, as the agency in charge of all socialized recorded thoughts.

Hence, as per model functions listed by Dr. Ranganathan, a public library has educational, informational, political, economic, industrial, cultural, and antiquarian objectives.

Functions of public library

The public library performs different functions to achieve its objectives. These functions can be listed as:

1. Supporting Education : The public library provides all kinds of information sources to the member of community, it serves, It helps people in educational endeavor whether formal, informal or non-informal education. It is especially, a boon for the people who acquire knowledge through non-formal and informal education system. Its services to the community support adult Education and social Education which ultimately demolishes illiteracy from the society. Because of this function, the public library is considered people's University.

2. Knowledge preservation and dissemination : The public library preserves the socio-cultural, historical, and geographical and categories of knowledge either produced or needed by the community, it serves.

3. Creating Reading Habits and love for knowledge : The public library provides all kinds of reading materials such as books, periodicals, popular magazines, etc which creates reading habits among the people of the community, and has positive effects on creating responsible citizens.

Basic Elements of public libraries

1. A Free library : A public library does not charge its users any fee for any of its services like consultation of books on its premises or loan of books for home reading or for rendering reference service or for providing recreation through a film show or any other cultural program. Thus, a public library is unique in bestowing a right to every citizen to have free access to its books and other information resources.

2. Financed by public finds : The finance needed for the establishment, maintenance and development of public libraries is secured mostly public funds. That is, the government under the law of the land levies an indirect tax known as library cess, which is levied as surcharge on property land possessed by a person on income accursed on professions or vocations or a vehicles owned by a person. As money accessed by way of library cess may not be sufficient for establishment, maintenance and development of public libraries, the state governments in some cases contribute certain amount to the library fund.

3. An auxiliary Educational institution : Over the centuries civilized society has evolved a number of educational institutions of formal learning like schools, colleges and universities. But, as the students' population, which is increasing every year, is physically spread out in cities, towns and villages, the academic libraries are unable to meet all their demands. So the public libraries located in these localities assist the students/teachers by providing suitable educative material as may be needed to successfully complete their formal education with ease.

4. A Mandatory Institution : A free supported by public funds in order to provide free access to every citizen impartially needs to be established under the law of the land by a competent authority like the parliament or the state assembly. In a democratic welfare nation it should be legally ensured that a public library is established, maintained and developed in all localities, so as to enable a citizen to reap the benefits, whatever free access to information, education and culture could bring. Thus, in the recent past almost every civilized nation has enacted a library law under the provisions of which public libraries have come into existence. The notable public libraries in India are Delhi Public Library, Delhi, Khuda Baksh Oriental Public, Patna, Connemara Public Library, Chennai.

1.4.2. Academic library

Education is a process of learning, with the aim to

develop the capabilities in the people at all levels. In this process schools, colleges and universities play a vital role in order to achieve the goals and objectives of the modern educational setup, libraries and self-learning have been considered vital components and integral parts of the entire educational process. Considerable thought and attention have been given to the planning and development of academic libraries at all levels. Education and library are two faces of the same coin. One cannot exist without the other. Hence, an academic library is an integral part of any institution of formal education. It supports the teaching-learning process research and other educational functions related to their parent institutions. The library collection is developed depending upon the nature of the institution and its academic programmes. The students, teachers, research scholars, administrative staff and other staff members of the institution are the users of the academic library. The needs of these users dominate the collection of an academic library. The number, qualities and qualifications of the library staff of an academic library differ on the basis of the type of academic library, its users, and the services it provides. The various types of academic libraries can be shown with the following chart:

Academic Libraries

School library	*College library*	*University library*
Primary school lib.	Junior college library	Conventional university lib.
Middle school library	Degree college library	Institutes of S & T library
Secondary school lib.	Postgraduate library	IIT library
Higher sec. school library	Professional college library	Agriculture University
Polytechnics	Medical University	IIM library

Objectives of an Academic library:

- To serve the needs of the academic community
- To collect and store all kinds of reading and reference material.

- To provide all kinds of informational materials to support the curricular requirements of the institute.
- To provide reading rooms for users.
- To render lending service appropriate to students, teachers and researchers.
- To provide responsive reference and information services.

School library : The school library is a library attached to or associated with as school to support the education system of the school. It caters to all the informational needs of the students, teachers and other staff of the school. There are four levels of school libraries corresponding to four levels of schools namely, primary, middle, secondary and higher secondary. The government and the agencies responsible for developing and supporting school education in India, have a policy that the school of all levels should be supported by a school library.

Objectives of school library:

- To Support the education programs of the school
- To awaken and foster interest in reading books and create reading habits among students.
- To nature good moral values and principals in students to create refined and responsible citizens.
- To develop self-learning skills and interest in using library for solving problems.
- To provide information further study and vocation.
- To help teachers to improve their teaching skills,
- To inculcate communication skills through extra-curricular activities like story -telling, viewing and discussions on audio-visual programs, workshop etc.

Functions of school library : The school library of all levels should develop the collection of information material to satisfy the objectives outlined by the type of school library. Apart from developing suitable collection of books and other material related to inspiration, information and recreation books and other materials, the school library is supposed to perform the following functions.

a. Lending of books and other materials.

b. Reading rooms with suitable furniture and lighting.

c. Reference services.

d. Guidance, counseling and advisory services.

e. News paper clipping services.

College library : College performs an important function in the educational process. College education provides a totally different environment for the students to go for higher studies. The library associated with college caters to the informational needs of the college community-students teachers, staff of the college and alumnus. The library help in the expansion of knowledge and satisfy the quest for knowledge of the users. Thus, college library is the automatic choice for students to supplement their classroom teaching. The support of a library at the college level is essential to broaden the minds of the young students to meet new challenges.

Objectives of college library

The chief objectives of a college library are:

- To give student community a wider and deeper understanding of the various disciplines.
- To help in all educational programs of the college.
- To prepare the more precious students for advanced studies in various disciplines.
- To provide guidance to students for higher studies and self-learning.
- To prepare the students for shouldering higher responsibilities in govt., depts., civic organizations,

commercial establishments, business and industries etc.

- To train them to become more enlightened, knowledgeable ad responsible citizens.
- To prepare them for varied professions like law, medicine, engineering, technology etc.
- To provide adequate and comfortable physical facilities.
- To provide bibliographical information and study, special materials for the research students of faculty.
- To keep faculty informed with the latest developments and updates in their respective subjects.

For translating into practice all these objectives, the college library has a central role to play.

Functions of college library

The major functions of a college library can be listed as:

I. Developing collection of textbooks, books of general knowledge reference materials and audio-visual materials to support educational and instructional programs of the college.

II. Procuring popular news-papers, Magazines and scholarly Journals to support students and teachers in acquiring deeper knowledge of their subject area.

III. Making the library resources accessible through proper classification, cataloging ad shelving.

IV. Providing physical facilities such as functional building, furniture, equipment, reading rooms etc.

V. Developing collection of aspiratory materials like fiction, poetry, biographies, travel-books etc

VI. Organizing orientation programs for new students to make them aware of the facilities and resources available in the library.

Key components of an Ideal College Library

The following are the key components that make a efficient college library system:

- A balanced collection of books and other learning and teaching materials including wide range of reference and textbooks.The quality of the collection has to be determined on the basis of a well thought-out acquisition policy. This policy is usually laid down by the library Advisory committee headed by the college principal where librarian is the member secretary.
- The user community, comprising students, teachers, the college management and other getting standard library services.
- Physical facilities like building, furniture, equipment in a separate college library building which is very attractive and functional.
- Professional staff of the library with high academic and professional qualification and experience.
- The college management.
- Finance and Budget while the Radhakrishana Commission recommended the setting a part of the six percent of the total college budget for the development of the respective libraries which was raised to (10) ten percent by Kothrai Commission.

College library services:

Important college library services are:

- Provide reading, lending and textbook services.
- Guide students in the use of manual or computer catalogue
- Provide information, reference and referral services to all library members.
- Display new books and lists of multiple media material.

- Documentation services, current awareness service, special journals, Indexing/Abstracting service etc.
- Reprographic and inter-library loan service.
- Audio-visual services.
- Exhibitions and special displays.
- Train and instruct students to use library resources in a effective and efficient manner.

University libraries

A library is more important in a University, because a library can do without a University where as a University cannot function without a library. The number of universities in India has gone up from a mere twenty in 1947 to more than five hundred at present. Today, university libraries have a very large and difficult role to play in order to meet a variety of demands of information and knowledge by far larger number of students. Thus, university library is an integral part of a university. The academic programmes of a university cover a wide range of disciplines and subjects. Hence, a library becomes an essential component of the university to support its academic and research activities. Because of the responsibilities a university library shoulders it is considered the heart of a university around which teaching and research revolves. According to the Association of University teachers the prime function of the university library is to provide facilities for study and research for the members of its own institutions. A University library assists the university n five major functions such as teaching and learning, research and generation of new knowledge, dissemination and publication of research results; conservation of knowledge and ideas and extension programmes. The university libraries have to play a very challenging and difficult role to satisfy the demands of larger group of students, research scholars, member of the various academic and executive bodies of the management administrative and professional staff of the university

Objectives of a University Library : A university plays a very important role by supporting and helping the university in achieving its aims and objectives. It has to cope with the multi-dimensional activities of the university. The main objectives of a university library are:

- To provide intellectual and managerial leadership to the various fields of government, industry, health, engineering, law defense, education, agriculture etc. ad imbue them with a sense of social purposes.
- To train a band of research workers in all the areas mentioned above so that the results of research could be harnessed to improve the quality of life the people.
- To conserve knowledge and ideas for posterity.
- To foster the ideals of social justice, religions, tolerance national integration among its diverse people.
- To provide facilities for all teaching, learning, educational and research programs of the university.
- Satisfy informational needs of the students, teachers and researchers of the university.
- To provide latest knowledge to the teachers in their area of teaching and research.

Functions of a university library : University libraries support and help the university in achieving each of the objectives of the university. The major functions that are derived from these objectives are:

- Develop collections on a wide range of subjects for learning, teaching, research, publications etc
- Organize and store the library collections with proper classification, cataloguing, shelving etc to make the collections easily accessible to the users.

- Acquire materials such as books, journals, periodicals, newspapers and other sources of information to provide latest information and knowledge on the concerned subjects.
- Provide reference, information and documentation services to the university community to keep them up-to-date in their area of study and research.
- Keep pace with the development in the library management system and application of new technologies to provide better library services to the users.
- Learning and teaching
- Research and generation of new knowledge.
- Dissemination and publication of research results.
- Conservation of knowledge and ideas.
- Extension services.

Services of a University library : The university library should offer a number of library documentation and information services. The services ought to be planned, keeping in view the general demand for such services and the capability of the library in offering those services. User needs and interests are of primary concern in offering library services. The major services of university library include:

(a) Library Services :

1. Lending
2. Information and reference
3. Reading room
4. Assistance in the use of the library and
5. Display of current additions.

(b) Current Awareness Services (CAS) :

1. Current contents of Journals.
2. Alerting services to important literature in selected fields.

   3. Selective dissemination of information (SDI) and
   4. Newspaper clipping services.

(c) Bibliographic Services :
   1. Literature search.
   2. Compilation of Bibliographies in specific topics and
   3. Index to current literature

(d) Condensation services :
   1. Preparation of Abstraction on specific topics.
   2. Digest services.
   3. Preparation of reviews/progress/advances on specific subjects
   4. State-of-Act reports.

(e) Specialized Services :
   1. User Education.
   2. Exhibition and special displays.
   3. Special lectures and demonstrations and
   4. User oriented seminars, workshops.

(f) Other Services :
   1. Document supply Services.
   2. Reprographic Services.
   3. Translation services and
   4. Computer based information retrieval.

Special library

Special libraries are a natural outcome of the need for information support to research and development, business and industry, expanded functions of governments and similar other organizations. The special libraries are established to meet the informational requirements of the organizations they are associated with. Such organizations are devoted to Research and Development (R&D) activities. The special library procures all types of information sources such as handbooks, technical reports, state-of-the-art reports, bibliographies, current awareness bulletins, periodicals, indexes, projects of the organization.

Definition of Special Library : Though the concept of special library is of a recent origin, a good number of experts have defined the special library. "Librarians Glossary of Terms" by M.L.M Harrod defines that a 'Special library is a collection of books and other printed, graphic or recorded material dealing with a limited field of knowledge and provided by a learned society, research organization, industrial or commercial undertaking, government department or even an educational institution. It may also be a special branch of a public library serving certain interests or occupational groups such as a technical library or a special subject library, meeting the needs of all enquires on that given subject such as music library." The American Library Association's (ALA) Glossary of library and information science defines special library as, "a library established, supported and administrated by business firms, private, corporations, associations, government agencies, or other special interest groups or agencies to meet the information needs of its members or staff in pursuing the goals of the organization. The scope of services is limited to the subject interest of the host or parent organization."

Broadfield defined that "a special library is neither academic, commercial, national nor public, but it intends to serve the needs of a portion of a community requiring detailed information on a limited subject field." Dr. S.R. Ranganathan, a renowned library scientist prefers to call it as specialist library to supply detailed information regarding some subject field scientific, technical and otherwise. A special library serves specialist users, located within a single organization or group and is responsible for the collection, organization, storage, retrieval and dissemination of information directly concerned and ancillary to the work of the specialized institutions with which it is attached.

Objectives and purpose of Special Libraries

While other types of libraries serve multiple objectives such as education, research, recreation, cultural and social activities. The major and perhaps only objective of a special library is the provision of information, in support of the objectives of its parent organizations. The purposes of special libraries are usually other than provision of education or conventional library services, invariably meeting the information requirements of the organization to which they are attached. Special libraries are established in R&D establishments, Govt. departments, directories, industrial and business undertakings, learned societies and professional associations, trade and business association's hospitals and health services, social and welfare organizations museums, national gallery of art etc. However, special libraries are also established to serve a particular group of users or specialists working on a subject or a group of subjects or on a particular type of documents etc.

The following table illustrates the special aspects of special libraries.

Distinguish Aspects	*Special library*
Special user groups	Libraries for the Doctors, Entrepreneurs, industrialists, Engineers etc.
Kind of Activity	Nutrition (library of the National Institute of Nutrition, Hyderabad, Medicine (Medical Library) parliament library, central secretariat library.
Special in a group of subject	Food science and technology (The library of the central food and Technological Research Institute, Mysore.
Types of Document	A film library, a video cassette library, a manuscript library.

A few specialized objectives of a special library are:

- To develop current as well as respective collections of information in core subjects based on the projects and programs of the parent organization.
- To provide promptly the latest information about the significant developments in the field wherever requested by the users.
- To provide all types of academic, technical and documentary support to render appropriate services of the specialists.

Functions of Special Library : A special library is a power house for the generation, storage and use of information. The major functions of special library are:

- To select, procure, organize, store and retrieve current information required by the researchers and other users of the library.
- To analyze synthesize and evaluate available information in the area of concern.
- To provide state of the art reports, critical reviews, monographic, research programs of the organization.
- To provide indexes, abstracts and extracts for critical analyses of literature, and identifying and procure relevant source of information.
- To provide reference service such as Current Awareness Services (CAS) Selective Dissemination of information (SDI) and translation Services.
- To provide accession lists, bulletins, news-letters, summaries, handbooks and manuals.
- To provide reprints, bibliographies and reference.
- To provide document Delivery Service including lending and inter-library loan service.

Services of special Library

a. Reference services

b. Current Awareness and Routing services.

c. Anticipatory services

d. Retrieval services.

e. Publication of Bulletins

f. Personal and Staff.

National Library

The National Library is the apex library in the library system of a country. It is usually created a fresh or entrusted the responsibility of National library by the constitutional provision of the country. The concept of National library is a recent development dating back to a few centuries. This development has been a feature of socio-economic culture and scientific advancement in the Western Industrially advanced countries. In other words, it is the outcome of the Renaissance and Reformation movements in Europe. Their growth has been accelerated by advances in science and technology and their applications in industry trade, transportation and communication. The national library of any country is the Custodian of the Intellectual heritage of the country. The intellectual heritage is the total information and knowledge wealth either produced within the nation, written by the national outside the country, and written by anyone on that particular Nation. Thus, National libraries collect and preserve the nation's literature. A National library is a library specifically established and funded by the government of a country to serve as the pre-eminent repository of information of that country. Most National libraries receive, by legal right (or copyright, or deposit), one free copy of each book and periodical printed in the country.

Definition of National library : Horrod's Librarians Glossary and Reference Book (1987) defines National library as a "library maintained out of government funds and serves the nation as a whole. The Books are mainly for reference. They usually receive material through legal deposit legislation are usually copyright libraries. The function of such a library is to collect and preserve for posterity all published records viz book, periodicals, newspapers and other printed and multimedia material of the country's cultural heritage. This is best done by a law requiring publishes to deposit copies of all publications produced by them and by purchasing books o their country published in other countries. A legal deposit normally has patently clauses to enable the act to be enforced." The ALA Glossary of library terms simply defines the National library as "a library maintained by a Nation." A more comprehensive definition of a National library has been given by UNESCO; in 1970 which is as under:

Libraries which, irrespective of the titles, are responsible for acquiring and concerning copies of all significant:

I. Publication published in the country and functioning as a

II. Deposit library either by law or under other arrangements

III. Produce a national Bibliography.

IV. Hold and keep up-to-date a large representative collection or foreign literature, including books about the country.

V. Act as a national bibliographical information Centre,

VI. Compile union catalogues;

VII. Publish retrospective Bibliographies.

This definition is quite comprehensive and covers all of the important functions of a national library. The legal provision is usually incorporated in the copyright laws of the country, by which an author, an artist or a musician, has the exclusive right, granted by law, for a certain number of years to make and dispose copies of literacy, musical or artistic work. These laws provide for the government to receive a few copies of print and non-print materials which are usually deposited with the National library, under special laws. e.g. the Delivery of

Books and Newspapers (public libraries) Act of the government of India. National libraries that enjoy this privilege are also known as copyright or legal deposit libraries.

Objectives of National Library : The major objectives of a National library are:

(i) To procure all the literacy output of that nation by the legal provision of the nation or other arrangement.

(ii) To acquire foreign literature about that nation.

(iii) To preserve the literacy wealth of that Nation for posterity.

(iv) To disseminate procured and preserved information through different services and publications.

(v) To maintain the national bibliography and publish it,

(vi) To coordinate with other libraries of the country to develop national library system.

Functions of a National library : In the final report of the Regional seminar on the development of National library in Asia and Pacific Area held at Manila in 1964, the following function of the National library have been given.

1. To provide leadership among the nation's libraries.
2. To serve as a permanent depository for all publications issued in the country:
3. To acquire other types of materials,
4. To provide bibliographical services.
5. To serve as a co-ordination Centre for cooperative activities and
6. To provide service to government.

Besides, to these functions, UNESCO's definitions also cover major functions of the National library. Examples of some national libraries are:

- National Agricultural Library India,
- National Musical Library India,
- National Science Library India,
- National Library of Canada Co-operative Activities.

Descriptive Account of a Few National libraries

A National library performs wide ranging functions and activities which are at the Centre of the Nation's bibliographical activities. Against this background, profiles of the National library of India, the United States of America and United Kingdom are given below:

The National library of India

The National library of India, Kolkatta, is the apex body of the library of India. Serving as a public library, it is a permanent repository of all documents published in India, After the independence of India, The National library came into being in place of imperial library by the "Imperial library (change of Name) Act in 1948. It was accorded special status of on Institution of national importance in the Article 62 in the 7th Schedule of the Union list of the constitution of India and Maulana Abdul Kalam Azad, the union minister of Education opened the library to public on 1st February 1953. Founded as Calcutta public library in 1835 and was opened to public on 21st March 1836. Later Lord Curzon, the viceroy and Governor General of India merged this library with the official imperial library consisting of Government Departmental libraries and the remnants of the East India company library. With this nucleus, Lord Curzon declared open the new Imperial library of India on 30th January 1903 in the Metcalf Hall. John Malfarlane of the British Museum was invited to look after the new imperial library, as its first librarian. The Imperial library also had a galaxy of great librarians, such as Harinath De, John Alexander Chapman, K.M Asadullah, a good organizer and administrator, who had the credit of starting library training courses in 1935 in the Imperial library, Shri, B.S Kesaven, a man of vision, enthusiasm and administrative skill was appointed the first librarian of the new National library in 1948.

Services of National library of India, Kolkatta: The National library extends its services through its various reading rooms, lending sections, bibliography and reference divisions. Presently the following services are offered.

- Lending including inter library loan.
- Reading Rooms
- Reading and reference services.
- Bibliography and Reference services.
- Reprography services.
- Indian library Review, A blog
- Services for children
- Training and Guidance

(A) *Lending Services* : A peculiar feature of the National library of India is that except for rare books, gift collections, generally out-of-print publications, governments and UN documents and serials, all other books are let out for home reading. This function is rather peculiar to a National library as mot National libraries are for reference only and seldom offer lending services to individual users. However, for historical reasons, the National library of India has continued its lending facilities to the member of the library in and out of Kolkatta. On an average 250 books are issued everyday out of 2.2 million collections

(B) *Reading Rooms* : Apart from its main reading room which accommodates 320 readers at a time, the National library maintains ten reading rooms for using different specialized materials. The main reading room stocks a very selective and open shelf collection of about 10,000 volumes of general reference books and books for basic study and reference, a specific field of knowledge.

(C) *Bibliographic and Reference Service* : The Bibliography Division of the National library was established in 1951 with an aim to function as an active agent to disseminate knowledge and information in an organized and effective manner. This service is offered in response to requests from scholars, researchers and writers for a bibliography on a specific topic, without any charge for the service. These bibliographies are usually short and selective list of translations and list of bibliographies published in India are compiled and sent to the UNESCO for inclusion in the India translation. The Indian National Bibliography, a monthly record of India books, is compiled and published by the Central Reference Library. Reference service is offered to persons who visit the library in person as well as to those who make enquires through telephone or post.

(D) *Reprography Service* : With the installation of Plain paper copiers at the main and other reading rooms, facilities are provided for obtaining copies of journal articles, small technical reports, etc, at nominal rates to scholars and research workers. Anin-house printing unit is operating for printing small documents for limited circulation.

1.11.6. The library of Congress (LC)

The library of congress is the largest library in the world, with millions of books, recordings, photographs, newspapers, maps manuscripts in its collections. Today's library of congress is an unparalleled world resource. The collection of more than 167 million items includes more than 39 million catalogued books and printed in 470 languages, more than 72 million manuscripts, the largest rare book collection in the world, are the world's largest collection of legal materials, films, maps, sheet, music and sound recordings. The library of Congress, Washington, D.C which is at present considered as the national library of the United States of America, was originally created to serve the U.S Congress. It was established in 1800 and by the copyright law of 1870, the library acquired the states of a depository library. Today the library ranks as one of the largest national libraries of its kind and occupies an eminent place in the world of scholarship and learning. The library of congress occupies three building on Capitol Hill. With 71 areas, 4800 staff members. The Thomas Jefferson Building (1897) is the original separate library of congress building. The John Adans Building was built in 1938 and the James Madison Memorial Building was completed in 1981. With the mere collection of 3000 volumes in the beginning (1814) today library has more than 167 million items on approximately 830 miles of bookshelves. The library receives some 15,000 items each working day and adds approximately 12,000 items to the collection daily. The library houses the largest book with a 5-by-7 foot book featuring color images of Bhuton and the smallest book in the library is 'old King cole' with its 1/25 × 1/25, or about the size of the period . The library preserves and provides access to a rich, diverse, and enduring source of knowledge to inform, inspire and engage on the intellectual and creative endeavours.

Organization of Library of Congress : The chief executive of library of congress is the librarian, a top ranking government official, appointed directly by the president of the United States, vested with enormous powers and responsibilities. The librarian is assisted by top ranking professional library experts, scholars, and specialists. The library is itself organized into eight major blocks or departments. They are:

- Office of the librarian
- Management Services.
- Congressional Research Service
- Copyright office
- Law library

- Processing Services
- Research Services
- National programs
- Each of these eight departments are organized into divisions and sections based upon users, served, functions performed materials acquired/processed services, rendered programs formulated and implemented.

Service of Library of Congress : The basic purpose of its establishments was to serve the members of the Congress; personalized services are rendered to the members of the Congress. The law library services the legal community. The Research service cluster, comprising divisions for performing arts, Area Studies, General Reference Special collection and preservation-serves, for the scholar and academic community. The creative world of authors, writers, musicians, artists, etc are served by the copyright division. The National progress Cluster serves many national programs such as the American Floklife Centre, National library service for the blind and physically Handicapped, Educational liaison office, publishing office and others. Within these five major departments nearly 90 independent functions are performed including several reading rooms wherein 3000 persons can set at a time.

National library Activities of Library of Congress : The library of Congress performs various activities which are national and international in scope and perception. The National Union catalogue, the cataloguing-in-publications project and the library automation program, the computerization of library of Congress which is generally known as the Machine Readable Cataloguing (MARC) project are some major National level activities of the Library of Congress. The MARC project also contributed to international thinking on the subject of machine Readable cataloguing and set international standard formats for cataloguing various types of documents. The National union catalogue (NUC)complied, maintained and printed by library of Congress is an index to world publications and considered to be a valuable service to scholarly and library communities. Libraries of Congress's computer activities for library automation and Machine Readable bibliographical records have been a pacesetter and precursor to many international computerized programs in libraries. The library of congress is indeed a highly complex institution but a vibrantly active Centre. Endowed with such incomparable facilities and unparalleled riches it is no wonder that scholars all over the world regard the library as a heaven for their academic pursuits.

The British Library

The British Library is the National library of the United Kingdom. It has the world's leading resources for scholarship, research and innovation, with incomparable collection, and expertise of staff. It reflects the intellectual, cultural, and socio-economic life of the country. The library aims to serve scholarship, research and development industry, commerce and all other major users of information. The British Library was established in 1973 by an act of parliament (1972). It brought together the library departments of the British Museum; the British National bibliography limited and in 1974, the functions of the office for scientific and technical information (DSTI). Subsequently, the library took responsibility for other organizations, viz, the Indian office library and Records in 1982, The HMSO, Binderies in 1982 and the National sound Archive in 1982. The Library has a collection of 15 million items and about 3 million new items are added every year.

Objectives of the British Library : The objectives of the British library as depicted in the white paper are as follows:

a. Preserving and making available for reference at least one copy of every book and periodical of domestic origin and of as many overseas publications as possible. The aim will be to provide as comprehensive a reference service as possible.

b. Providing an efficient central lending and photocopying service in support of other libraries and information systems of the country, and

c. Providing central cataloguing and other bibliographic services related not only to the needs of the central library but to those of libraries and information centers throughout the country's in close co-operation with central library's overseas.

Functions of the British library : The British library act specifies the following functions of the British library:

I. The British library shall constitute a comprehensive collection of Books, manuscripts, periodicals, films and the recorded matter, whether printed or otherwise.

II. The library shall act as a National Centre for reference, study and Bibliographical and other information services in relation to scientific and technological matters and to the humanities, and

III. The services of the library shall be available in particular to institutions of education and learning, other libraries and industry.

IV. The library will carry out and sponsor research and in this way it will benefit institutions providing library and information facilities whether public or otherwise.

Organization and services : The British library is directed by a Board of Management comprising of the Chairman, the Chief Executives, The Director Generals from the three operating divisions (Humanities & Social Sciences, Science & Technology, and Industry) and nine members who have knowledge and experience of library or university affairs, finance, industry or administrative. The public service unit provides a wide range of reference and information services. This unit is responsible for the General Reading Room, Rare Books, official publications and social sciences, library Association library and Newspaper library. The special collections unit looks after the non book collections within the library that includes western manuscripts. The Science, Technology and industry division not only provides service to science, technology and industry but also supplies documents to the humanities and social science communities. The document supply Centre is the largest such Centre in the world, exclusively devoted to the supply of documents on loan photocopy and micro-film. The science reference and information services unit provides reference and information services covering modern science and technology, business and commerce, patents, trade-marks, and designs. The Bibliographic service division creates a National database, recording UK publishing output. It publishes a range of printed and microfiche bibliographies including the British National Bibliography and books in English, operates BLAISE (British Library Automated Information Service) online service which access to the British library and other complimentary databases for Information retrieval and record supply. Under British library Research and development division, it promotes and awards funds for research and development related to library and information operations in all fields, relating to library, documentation and information aspects. Numbers of one-line access service are provided also. The serial, conference and monographic files are on the unity system. The literature files are available on BLAISE. The JOURNAL COTENTS PAGE Service is available on subscription NEW TITLE ALERT, is a weekly listing of new journal title. The stock alert service offers subject searches based on BLAISE collections.

1.5. FIVE LAWS OF LIBRARY SCIENCE

The five laws of library science were enunciated in 1928 by Dr. Shiyali Ramamritra Ranganathan (S.R. Ranganathan, 1892-1972), the librarian of the University of Madras. He made several significant contributions to the library profession. He formulated the five laws of library science in 1928 and published them in his famous book entitled, "Five Laws of Library Science' in 1931. He owes the first law to Prof. Edward N. Ross, his mathematics teacher. The laws of library science govern various disciplines within the field of library science. These laws are the most influential concept in the field of library science. They are fundamental and discuss the basic philosophy of library science. They concisely represent the ideal services and organizational philosophy of all types of libraries, even today. These laws provide scientific basis and general principles which serve as guidelines to librarians in organizing and managing information products and services. In other words, these laws make library organization, management and operation efficient and universalize its services. Every activity relating to library services has a rationale in one or another of these laws or in all of them collectively. The laws, therefore, constitute the philosophical basis for all library work, programs, activities and services. The five laws of library science given by Dr. S.R. Raganathan are:

- Books are for use
- Every Reader his/her book.
- Every book its reader.
- Save the time of reader.
- The library is a growing organism.

First law Books are for use

The first law of library science is "Books are for use" which is simple and states a self evident truth. Historically, in the 15th 16th century periods, books were chained to the shelves and the emphasis was on preservation rather than on use. At later stage, books were made available to those people, who paid a fee, but with the onset of post-industrial society, the concept of modern library came into being. The library is now regarded as a service institution to serve the social information needs of its users. Ranganathan did not reject the motion of preservation and storage, but asserted that the purpose of such activities was to promote the use of books. Modern libraries are attractive, comfortable and a number of special services are introduced to ensure optimum utilization of books. Libraries take initiatives to make the library a Centre of intellectual achievements by increasing the use of books. By emphasizing on the use of books, the law stress upon access related issues such as location, building, library hours, book selection, library staff etc.

Implication of the first law

In order to satisfy the first law of library science, libraries have to look into a number of factors. The most prominent are:

a. Library Location : A library must be located in the midst of its user if it is a public library; it should be located in the heart (centre) of the city. If it is an academic library it would be wise to locate it centrally to enable accessibility to all the students. A centrally located library will be helpful in increasing the use of books. The point to be kept in view is the easy accessibility of the library to its users.

b. Library Hour's : Another implication of this law is that the library hours should be convenient to users. School libraries, college libraries and public libraries are particularly carriers in this matter, for many of them are kept open when their clientele are engaged otherwise and are not able to visit the library. The opening hours of the library are according to the convenience of the library users. Now-a-days, due to the impact of information society, the majority of libraries are kept open round the clock. Opening and closing hours of the library should be adjusted to ensure maximum utilization of library resources.

c. Library Building and Library Furniture : The first law demands that proper attention should be paid to the planning and designing of the library building and to the various items of furniture provided in the building. The building should be functional and at the same time aesthetic. The furniture should also be functional and attractive. If the racks on which the books are kept are too high and the books on the top shelves cannot be easily reached, the use of books become difficult,. The implementation of the first law motivates us to provide open access to books to library users. The first law has, thus, exercised tremendous influence on the library building and its furniture.

d. Book Selection : The first law had a tremendous impact on book selection procedure. Book selection should meet the needs of the present and potential users. In order to maximize the use of books, the books should be selected in suitable informative, evaluative and inspiring way. In fact, the first law allows placing of only those books on the shelves which are regularly, read, enjoyed understood and acted upon. Worn out and out-of-date books should be weeded out from the library collection, from time to time.

e. Library Staff : The law states that to disseminate knowledge and to put the books to maximum use, the libraries must have highly qualified and professionally trained staff. Asserting the users to find and use library resources is the responsibility of the library staff, as most of the users do not know how to use the resources. To know the needs of the users, and teaching them use of library resources, is an essential task of library staff. The staff should cultivate service attitude towards readers. They should be courteous cheerful and helpful. "Service with a smile should be the motto. The credibility of the staff, in respect of their knowledge, ability and personal attitude to readers, is a crucial factor in the promotion of the use of books. In short, the implication of the first law is profound, rich, useful and revolutionary. This law has changed the concept of librarianship as it was in the olden days.

Second Law Every" Reader His/ Her Book"

The second law of library science has established a new concept of libraries and has inculcated the culture of libraries. Every reader his/her books means books for all instead of chosen few. If the approach of the first law is from "Books" point of view, the approach of the second law is from 'user' point of view. It emphasizes the availability of library services to every kind of reader, irrespective of age, sex, vocation, the capacity for self help and the ability to read. The second law states that every user of the library should get the book he/she wants. This law also advocates the generalization and democratization of library services. The second law supports the principal of equality of opportunity for books for all and provides a suitable environment for all to learn. Hence the law, 'Every Reader His/ Her Book' or 'Books are for all'.

1.13.2.1. Implications of the Second Law

The second law imposes certain obligations on the states, the library authority, the library staff and the Reader.

a. Obligation of the State : It is the obligation of the state to provide sufficient support to its citizens for informal, continuous self-education through the network of libraries. To meet this responsibility, the state has certain obligations. The first and the foremost is the library legislation, which makes adequate provisions regarding library cess, percentage of the cess to be collected from the people and grants to be given by the government for library system. The coordinated efforts strengthens, library resources though interlibrary loan, which enhances the efficiency and standard of service for the readers. Various levels of provisions for better functioning of libraries are as follows:

- State public library Act,
- State library Authority.
- Local Library Authority
- Local Library Committee and Village Library Committee
- State Central Library
- Finance, Accounts and Audit.

The law desires on integrated library grid (Horizontal and Vertical Levels) of public library system.

b. Obligation of the Library Authority : The library authority should monitor the functioning of libraries and the overall system. They should try to provide prompt and fee service. For the second law obligation of library authorities is in respect of choice of books and the choice of the staff. These are the main functions of authorities in libraries. To provide 'Every Reader his/her Book', the second law requires the libraries to know the subject, user needs and the language of the books used. The second law indicates that a library should select books on all the major occupations of its actual and potential users. The libraries should select and furnish books which satisfy the demands of the neo-literates as well as scholars; careful selection means to build up collection according to the tastes and interest of the readers. To exploit these resources, competent library staff is needed. Only the competent staff can satisfy the user's requirements, hence well qualified library staff should be recruited to facilitate and ensure 'every reader his/her book.'

c. Obligations of the Staff : The library staff has a

great role to play in the success of the second law. The second law directs the library authority to provide adequate and devoted staff to show every reader how to use books as tools. To act as the canvassing agent for the books, the staff must know the readers, must know the books and actively help every reader to find books of his or her interest. The second law also demands the staff to help the users of the libraries in locating the required books. Catalogue is another facility that second law demands. The catalogue is such a tool which reveals the hidden contents of such documents by cross reference entries and subject analytical entries. Otherwise, reader may not get this material in spite of best efforts. Besides, the open access system will satisfy the expectations of this law, which enables the reader to decide what he should read. If a reader is not satisfied with a particular books She/he Can choose another suitable book. Thus it will increase the chances for every reader to get the book of his/her choice. The second law demands of the staff give active help to readers to locate and use literature with the help of tools like bibliographies, indexing and abstracting services etc.

d. Obligations of the Reader : The reader also has certain responsibilities cast on him by the second law. It particularly wants him to observe the library rules in respect of loan and use of books. If a reader retains a book beyond the period of loan he is depriving other readers who may want to use the book. There are readers who misplace books with a view to monopolize their use. The result is a gross violation of the second law. The second law strongly advocates user education programs in libraries. The users of the library should cooperate with the library staff, so that the latter can provide better services.

e. Resource Sharing : Even with the best of efforts, it will not be possible to make a library self-sufficient. There would hardly be any library that is capable of ensuring every reader his book which points to the need for resource sharing among libraries. The resources of one library should be available to the other libraries brought into the resource sharing network. Efforts are made for promoting such resource sharing and other cooperative programs under the auspices of national and international agencies. This is an important step in the direction of satisfying the second law.

Third Law "Every Book its Reader"

The Third law stresses the maximum use of books by their readers. It urges that an appropriate reader should be found for every book. It is closely related to the second law, but it focuses on the book itself suggesting that each book in a library has an individual or a number of readers who would find that book useful. It is the duty of the library staff to bring the readers in contact with books. The law advocates on open access system, classified shelf arrangement, subject analytical entries, provision of reference services, publicity methods, extension services and book selection policy. Investment unused books is a dead divestment and a waste. This situation should be avoided.

Implication of the Third Law

a. Open Access : The open access system provides an opportunity to see and examine the book collection with as much freedom as one has in one's own library. The user is allowed to browse/select/choose books on the shelves on his/her own. It increases the use of the books. It provides an opportunity to its readers to search for books which they never expected to find due to various reasons with this specific support, less-used books are put to use. Open access, thus helps in achieving the Third Law.

b. Shelf Arrangement : The third law emphasizes the need to arrange the books on shelves in classified sequence based on their thought content. This arrangement brings books on the same subject together for easy browsing. If the shelf area is provided with well devised guide's ad labels the use of each item increases.

c. Easy Access : Another important factor helping every book to get its reader is that the books may be placed within the easy reach of the readers. The third law emphasizes that the height of the racks should not be more than the average height of the readers.

d. Catalogue : The library catalogue of the holdings gives useful bibliographical information about the library collection and helps in the selection of books. The third law also advocates that the library catalogue should play an important role to provide every book to its reader. Subject analytical entries help in finding readers for a suitable book. Series entries and subject cross reference entries also provide needed information of books to the reader. In alphabetical part of the catalogue all the entries having the same series as the subject are brought together.

e. Reference Service : The books cannot reach to the hands of readers unless their content is interpreted by the reference staff. It is the duty of a reference librarian to act like bridge/marriage makers between books and readers. They should find a suitable reader for every book or vice versa. They should also identify all those books which are of less use or no use. This is a kind of service that the third law experts from the reference.

f. Display of New Books : The newly added books to the library should be displayed as it enhances the chance of every book to find its reader. In this way, newly displayed books catch the attention of readers and are read by those who are interested in them.

g. Publicity : Publicity is a powerful tool to attract the users of the library and thereby to increases the chances for every book to find its reader. Regular publicity is given through library, bulletins, newspapers, magazines, printed catalogues, subject book lists, press notices, book fair, window displays, radio, / TV talk, public, lectures, exhibitions demonstration tours. Library week, broachers and leaflets. The library should adopt all authorized methods to attract more library users.

h. Book Selection : The third law has an important role in the book selection process. For satisfying the third law and fulfilling the users demand it, it is essential to examine the users, requirements and the objectives of the library. Book selection must be proper, timely and based on the local demand, local history and local needs of the users. Thus, the book selection process plays an important role in satisfying the third law of library science.

i. Extension service : The extension service is a vital part of the implication of the third law. The purpose of providing extension services is to convert the library into a social Centre for encouraging and inculcating reading habits and to turn a non-reader into a regular reader.

To satisfy the demand of the third law, librarians celebrate local festivals and certain national days dedicated to national leaders or ideas, an participate in local festivals in India, where such celebrations attract huge crowds, this form of extension service has a great potential to satisfy some aspects of the third law of library service.

Fourth law save the time of the Reader

This law requires that there should be no time lag between the demand received from the user and the document supplied. This law makes its approach from the point of view of the user. Readers coming to the library are busy people and they should not be made to wait longer than necessary to get their needs met. They should get an exact and fast service from the library. In many individuals, intellectual interest may exist only momentarily and unless it is satisfied at the moment of its existence, it may vanish. The objective of this law is to save the time of the reader.

Implication of the Fourth Law

a. Open Access : The fourth law advocates open access. In closed system, readers do not have access to books directly and a lot of time is spent in this system. There is both objective time and subjective time which are wasted. But, in open access system, the reader is engaged in handling and perusing the books himself/herself and he is not conscious of the passage of time. So a lot of his subjective time is saved, if the books are properly arranged and there is no misplacement his objective time is also saved. So, Open Access is an effective means of satisfying the fourth law.

b. Classified Arrangement : The classified arrangement of books in the stack room saves the time of the readers, as it is easy for a reader to find all books on the same subject arranged at one place for browsing. The arrangement of entries in the catalogue cabinet in classified manner, aids the reader to select the books easily from the respective shelves. The fourth law, therefore, calls for classified arrangement of books in the stack room.

c. Stack Room Guides : Proper signal guides in the stack room save the time of the user. It may be quite useful to place them at the entrance of the stack room. Every book shelf must have a separate signal guide.

d. Shelf Arrangement : The comfortable and useful method of shelf arrangement can save significant time of the user. Arrangement by subject has been found to be useful as it makes it easy for the reader to locate the desired book.

e. Catalogue : The fourth law acknowledged the composite nature of the books. Some prominent aspects of the composite book can be highlighted only by cross-reference and analytical entries. To save the time of the reader, the library catalogue is generally divided in two parts Alphabetical and classified. Although, the library catalogue enables a reader to locate the desired book without any of loss of time, yet it becomes difficult to search for a micro-document. Further to save readers time, the library must procure published bibliographies of individual authors, subject bibliographies, cumulative indexes to periodicals, national and regional bibliographies, union catalogues, computerized database.

f. Reference Service : The law supports that the library staff should provide adequate personal help to their readers, such as help is known as Reference Service. Most of the readers require such assistance in meeting their information needs. They can bring books and readers together by providing ready reference services. Reference staff can also help in the selection of books. Documentation services like indexing, abstracting, translation, Reprography, information service like CAS, SDI, referral service, information consolidation and repacking etc, helps in fulfilling the requirements of the fourth law. The message "Save the time of the reader" makes all necessary efforts to meet demands of the reader in least possible time with the help of reference cum guidance services.

g. Issue /Return Methods (Charging Systems) : Circulation service is an important service of library. If this service is well planned and equipped, it saves the time of both the user and staff. After a number of experiments, it is brought out that Browne Charging System, Newark Charging System, Ranganathan Reader Ticket-Book ticket method and Detroit self-charging system are some of the economical and time saving charging systems. The two-card systems found to save the time of the readers over Day Book and ledger system. Automated circulation system is better than all other systems that save the time of the users.

h. Other Services : To save the time of readers, libraries provide other services centralized/pre-natal cataloguing. The fourth law also deals with the time taken by the readers to reach the library. It should be so located as to save the time of the readers. The law demands setting up of the branch libraries and delivery stations for the same. Thus, this law deals with the different aspects of library policy and administration for reducing the time factor in all the library activities. The devices proposed in the law are the best classification and cataloguing system, open access, shelf arrangement, stack room guides, reference service and other. The basic objective of all such measures is to save the time of the reader.

Fifth Law Library is a Growing Organism

The fifth law is 'library is a growing organism'. The word organism instead of organization is significant for it underlines the characteristics of the library as a living institutional organism. It is important that we do not conceive of the library as a static entity, but as a dynamic growing entity. The basic components of a library are:

I. The book stock.

II. The staff

III. The readers, and

IV. The physical infrastructure i.e, the building, furniture and equipment.

When we say that a library grows, what we mean is that each of these components grows. Since library is trinity of books, Readers and staff, it is bound to grow in all three respects.

Implication of Fifth law

a. Book Stock/Collection : In the initial stags the growth of the book stock including periodicals would be fast. This has its impact on the sizes of the stack room, the catalogue cabinet and the catalogue room and the number of racks for accommodating the books. All these will necessarily have to grow in number and/or in physical dimensions. This would necessitate relabeling of shelves periodically.

b. Readers : The readers of the library are also bound to grow especially in a library that functions in keeping with the spirit of the fifth law of library science. This means that more space will be required.

c. Staff : Corresponding to the increase in book collection and the number of reader, new services will have to be introduced. Depending on the nature and interests of readers, the services will also have to be diversified. There will be a quantitative increase in administrative work and services and a qualitative diversification of services. These would necessitate an increase of staff of different levels both in the quantitative and qualitative sense.

d. Classification and the Catalogue : One important implication of the increasing intake of books on a variety of new subjects is that the classification scheme adopted should be hospitable to the subjects. The growth factor of a library also points to the need a catalogue, like the card catalogue, which would permit the interpolation of entries. So, the classification scheme should be comprehensive, all-embracing of all past and present issues and allowing space for any possible addition of knowledge. It means that the classification must be highly flexibly expandable and hospitable, so that it can accommodate any new subject without dislocating its pre-defined sequence.

e. Modernization : Libraries, especially the large ones, which grow fast in their size and services, may have to think of computerization of the various house-keeping jobs like the acquisition circulation, cataloguing, etc of books of libraries.

f. Weeding out of Books : Weeding out of Books of obsolete ones is necessary to adjust the new ones in the collection. Thus, the development and growth means weeding out of obsolete and unwanted books and adding new ones which are relevant and useful. Some librarians hold the view that after a stage of development, the number of books weeded out will equal the number of books added. This view gives rise to the concept of a self-renewing library.

g. Provision for the Future : Another important message of the physical growth of the library is that while planning and designing a library. There should be provision for the expansion of the building both horizontally and vertically. The need for more space often arises much sooner than anticipated and the lack of provision for expansion would block its development. The library building must have a self-sufficient system for adjusting books of fluctuating size.

Modern Interpretation of Five Laws

Dr. S.R. Ranganathan's Five Laws are so fundamental and farsighted that they are much valid and relevant in providing the right direction and an objective base to the changing dimensions of libraries. While knowledge and information have always been primarily instrumental in promoting material progress at every state of human society in the last fifty years that there has been amazing and spectacular developments in the access and availability of information and knowledge. The chief driving force of this development is information communication technology (ICTs) knowledge and information can be accessed today instantaneously, irrespective of its location and made available on a computer screen, downloaded and stored for future use. The bulk volume and variety in which information and knowledge are disseminated do not pose any problem of access and availability. The parameters alone have changed. It is, therefore, understandable that the five laws of library science restated substituting books with information and library with information systems, eminently fit in the new context of the changing society. The five laws can be related as:

- Documents/Information is for use.
- Every user his/her information.
- Every information its user.
- Save the time of the user.
- The documentation/Information system is a growing organism.

The first law "Information is for use" comprehends a whole range of the information transfer process stemming from the recognition that information is a basic impact that transforms a non-resources into a resource. Being itself such an important resource, information has to be harnessed, exploited and utilized in order to derive full benefit out of it. In other words the vital role of information in all national development is perceived in this law.

The second law "Every user his/her Information" suggests that the information needs of all users should be oriented to their exact needs. The second law points to a definite goal of organizing information systems and services, viz, optimum recall and precision in the provision of information. It stresses that the users are at the Centre in the design and operation of information systems.

The third law "Every Information its user" conveys that information created or generated should be focused on users. The familiar phrases "Right Information to the Right User" is Infact recapitulated here. The implication is that marketing and use of information are activities in tune with professional service.

The fourth law "Save the time of the User" and its corollary "Save the time of the Information professional," brings out the imperativeness to develop mechanisms for an information service that ensure maximum speed and effectiveness. In this context, modern information technology, helps to cut down delay and ensures efficiency and effectiveness.

The fifth law "The Information system is a growing organism" prescribes a system approach in developing information institutions with a self-adapting mechanism for meeting the dynamic needs of users of information. The five laws would serve very well in the self-driving multi-directional growth of information and have far-reaching dimensions. The organic growth of the multi-directional universe of information and the integration of information sources must result Ina matching growth of information institutions.

NOTE : In 1992, James R. Retting devised a sixth law as an extension of Ranaganthan's five laws. The sixth law is "*Every Reader His Freedom*". In 2004 AlirezaNoruzi applied Ranaganthan's five laws to the web in his paper Application of Ranganathan Laws to the web. They are:

- Web resources are for use.
- Every user his or her web resources.
- Every web resource its user.
- Save the time of the user.
- Web is a growing organism.

REFERENCES

1. Altay, Ahmet, Ammar Tekin, BachityahDursun(2012). The Role of the Libraries in the Information Society. Retrieved on 25-12-18 at *http://www.kirplareli.edu.tr/download//by-files/31796092.html*.
2. Central Board Of Secondary Education. Library and Information Science, Class XI, IstEd. 2014.
3. IGNOU (2011) BLIS-01 Development of Libraries and Their Role in Society. Block – 1. Library and Society, New Delhi, IGNOU.
4. IGNOU (2011). BLIS-01. Different types of Libraries and Their Functions. Block-7. Library and Society, New Delhi, IGNOU.
5. Khanana, J. K. (1994). Library and Society, 2nd Rev. Ed. New Delhi, Ess Ess Publications.

6. Kumar, P. S. G. (2003). Foundations of Library and Information Science. Delhi, B. R. Publishing Co.

7. National Institute of Open Schooling. Library and Information Science (NIOS). MODULE – 1 Library and Information Centers: Concept and Role in Society.

8. National Institute of Open Schooling. Library and Information Science (NIOS). MODULE – 1. Five Laws of Library Science.

9. Sahai, Shrinath (1973). Library and Community. New Delhi, Today and Tomorrow Printers and Publishers.

10. UNESCO'S Public Library Manifesto. Retrieved on 27-12-18 at *http://www.unesco.org/webworld/libraries/manifestos/libraman.html.*

2

Public Library System in India

2.1. INTRODUCTION

India celebrated its 66 years of Independence in 2013. A brief stock of its development in the library field help to introspect the progress made in the library field. An important landmark in the history of public library services in India was made by Maharaja Sayaji Rao Gaekward by introducing free compulsory elementary education backed by libraries in 1883 in the district of Baroda and thus free public library services in India were introduced as a system in 1907. It can, therefore, be traced out that 2007 is the centenary year of free public library services in India. In spite of several drawbacks, the public library system in India made considerable progress. According to Ramaiah, L.S. and Sankara Reddy, M. (2010), of 28 states and 7 union territories in India, only 17 states have enacted public library legislation. There are a total of 54,851 public libraries in India, of which, 30 state central libraries, 40 regional and divisional libraries, 364 district libraries, 4658 city/town libraries and 49,758 village libraries. A brief account of public library development is presented in the following paragraphs as a backdrop with a view to illustrate the sequence of happenings.

2.2. HISTORY OF LIBRARIES IN INDIA

A Public Library is regarded as the "People's University" as it caters to all sections of the public with information and supports the individuals in lifelong learning. As seen above most of the Indian states are offering free public library services, irrespective of public library legislation.

2.2.1. Ancient Period (before 1200 AD)

Education and libraries are intertwined. The history of the development of the public library may be said to be as old as that of education in India. During ancient times, the seekers of education stayed in the ashrams of gurus for several years. Many students joined ashrams from many neighboring countries. Oral tradition of education was imparted where writing was not available for much of the early times. Writing tradition came a little bit later. This is evident from the written and recorded materials found in India. In the Ashrams the manuscripts were kept for use of the teachers and students as well as for the visitors. Big ashrams were known as Vidyapeeths, where numbers of teachers are engaged to teach the students like modern universities. References are available to prove that Nalanda University (in Bihar) had its own multistoried library in 600 AD with massive collection of manuscripts. The collection of the library was housed in three buildings, each having nine floors and three hundred rooms. This library was opened by the then Emperor of India, King Davapal. The library was open for anybody that was known scholar and took interest in reading, interpreting and even copying the documents kept in the library. Chinese traveler Huen Tsang is known to have consulted this library in the seventh century and to have taken from here hundreds of treatises to China and Japan. This library was completely destroyed by Bakhtiar Khilaji, who invaded India in 1205 AD and burnt the library. Libraries in ancient India also developed at other famous centers of learning, such as *Vikramshila* and *Odantapuri.* Universities of ancient India, like Taxila and Vikramshala also have valuable collection on *Tantras* and manuscripts in their libraries.

2.2.2. Medieval period (1200-1757 AD)

Muslims ruled India in the Medieval Period and hence, it is also known as Mughal Period. All the succession of rulers, namely, Babur, Humayun, Akbar and Jahangir made their distinctive contributions to education and libraries. Babur established the first Mughal Imperial Library in 1526 and his son Humayun set up a library at Agra Fort with books, gilded pen cases, portfolios, picture books and beautiful works of calligraphy. After the death of Humayun, Akbar improved the management of library with some technical works and appointed calligraphers to copy good manuscripts. He also established a separate library for women at Fatehpur Sikri. Jahangir, another rule of Mughal period, made a law that when a wealthy man died heirless, the property should be used for building and repairing schools, monasteries, libraries, and other institutions, which helped the development of libraries in late medieval period. During this period the library staff had distinct designations like Nizam (head librarian) and Muhatin (Assistant librarian) and these were assisted by scribes, illustrators, calligraphers and copyists. During the late medieval period, Christian missionaries also contributed to the development of education and libraries.

2.2.3. The British Period (1757-1947)

Though the British came to India primarily to establish trade and commerce, a number of educational institutions and libraries were established during their rule. The University of Calcutta (1857), University of Bombay (1879), and University of Madras (1907) were the first three universities were established along with their libraries. There were only nineteen Universities in India before 1947. The British also showed keen interest to set up educational societies with their libraries and public libraries in India. The establishment of Bengal Royal Asiatic Society library (1784), Bombay Royal Asiatic Society (1804) and Calcutta Public Library (1835) enlightened the public. Some of the important libraries set up in 19th.Century in India are:

- Andrews Library, Surat(1850),
- Gaya Public Library, Gaya (1855),
- Long Library, Rajkot (1856),
- Connemara Public Library, Madras (1860),
- Government Library, Janagarh (1867),
- Adyar Library, Adyar (1886),
- Dahi Laxmi Library, Nadiad (1892).
- Gujarat Vernacular Society & library, Ahmadabad (1848),
- Barton Library, Bhavnagar (1882),
- Baroda State Library (1877),
- Cochin Public Library and Reading Room, Trichur (1873),
- Victoria General Library, Dhar (1856),
- Indore General Library (1852),
- Maharajah's Public Library, Jaipur (1899),
- Jammu and Kashmir library (1879),
- Kahtiawar library (1886), Kolhapur library (1850),
- Nizam's Dominion (1891), Travancore library (1829).

The Calcutta Public Library became Imperial Library in 1903 and later became the National Library of India after Independence. A very significant contribution to the public library movement in India was made by His

Highness the Maharaja Sayajirao III, Gaekwad of Baroda. He is remembered today as the "Father of Library Movement" in India. As education was the foundation to reconstruct a new social and economic life he introduced free and compulsory education in his princely states. Thus Baroda became the first state among the native states in British India to have compulsory free primary education. He also decided to establish library as an experiment in one of the towns with the State's financial assistance. In 1906, he went to America and studied the libraries there. He was very much impressed by the library services there for the development of the people in their social, economic and educational life and invited William Alanson Borden. Borden came to Baroda in 1910 and made a proposal for development of the best services of libraries in the State.

The Maharaja accepted Borden's proposal and a network of free public libraries consisting a state central library, four district or divisional libraries, forty-five town libraries, and more than a thousand village libraries was planned. Thus, Borden played a leading role for the establishment, management and organization of public libraries in India. Borden also conducted the first formal library-training programme in India at Baroda in 1911.

Dr S.R. Ranganathan also played a significant role in the library development as well as knowledge of library science. After joining the post of University Librarian at University of Madras in 1924, Ranganathan went to United Kingdom and gained knowledge on libraries. Ranganathan published his *Five Laws of Library Science* (1931), *Colon Classification* (1933) and *Classified Catalogue Code* (1934) and also prepared Model Public Library Bill, which helped to enact public library legislation in Indian states. Dr Ranganathan has made noteworthy contributions to the domain knowledge of library science through his 60 books and 2000 seminal research articles during his life time and has been revered as "Father of Library Science in India".

2.2.4. Post-Independence Period (1947 onwards)

Public libraries in India made a tremendous growth after the independence. The union and the state governments took considerable interest for the development of education and considered library as an essential part of it. To enhance the level of literacy of 16% in 1941, the government initiated some programs such as extension services, continuing education, social education, non-formal education and adult education. The public libraries played considerable role in the Community Development Projects that to accelerate the pace of socioeconomic development of the people.

The Delhi Public Library was established in 1951 under the joint auspices of UNESCO and Government of India to serve as a model public library for Asia. The public library legislation made its impact on the development of public libraries in India. The library movement helped to set up a number of private libraries in urban and rural areas initially, the public library legislation provided the public library services on a sound financial foundation with governmental support and library cess. The Kolhapur Public Libraries Act (1945) was the first library act in India and it was followed by Madras state (presently Tamil Nadu) in 1948, Andhra Pradesh (1960), Karnataka (1965), Maharashtra (1967), West Bengal (1979), Manipur (1988), Kerala (1989), Haryana (1989), Mizoram (1993), Goa (1994), Gujarath (2002), Odisha (2002), Uttaranchal (2006) and Rajasthan (2006). The Advisory Committee for Libraries (known as Sinha Committee) which was constituted in 1957 by the Government of India, a drafted Model Library Bill. Another Model Public Libraries Act was drafted by the Working Group on Public Libraries under Planning Commission in 1965; however, more than half of the states in India did not enact their own public library legislation. Under the provision of Public Libraries Acts, some of the existing prominent libraries were designated as the State Central Libraries of the respective states. Thus, the Connemara Public Library in Madras and Asafia Library in Hyderabad became the State Central Libraries of Tamil Nadu and Andhra Pradesh respectively.

In 1954, the Delivery of Book Act was passed and later amended in 1956 to include newspapers also. As per the Act every publisher in India obliged to deposit one copy each of its publications to the National Library in Calcutta, the Asiatic Society Library in Bombay, Connemara Public Library in Madras, and Delhi Public Library in New Delhi. Raja Rammohan Roy Library Foundation (RRRLF), an autonomous body under the Department of Culture, Ministry of Education, was established in 1972 with the main objective to promote and support public library movement in the country. Matching and non-matching grants are provided too many libraries by the Foundation to assist state library services in developmental works. In 1979, a library section was established in the Department of Culture under the Ministry of Education, Government of India with an objective was to promote the development of public libraries in India.

A Working Group on Modernization of Library Services and Informatics was appointed by the Planning Commission in 1983 to work out a National Policy on Library Services and Informatics. On the basis of the document prepared by RRRLF and another document prepared by Indian Library Association, the Ministry of Human Resources Development, Govt. of India set up Prof. D. P. Chattopadhyaya Committee in 1985 for the formulation of a National Policy on Library and Information Systems (NAPLIS). The Committee submitted its report in 1986. The Working Group on Libraries and Informatics appointed a subgroup on public libraries reviewed the public library services and recommended for library services to children, neo-literates, tribal groups, etc. In 1992, 73rd and 74th Amendments to the Indian constitution have been made to provide constitutional provisions relating to village Panchayats and municipalities. Accordingly, the Pachayats and municipalities may offer their public library services.

2.3. PROMINENT LIBRARIES IN MODERN INDIA

2.3.1. National Library, Kolkata

The National Library of India is located at Belvedere, Kolkata, West Bengal state and it has history of nearly two centuries. It was originally established in 1836 as Calcutta Public. Library and was running on a proprietary basis. The Governor General, Lord Metcalf transferred 4,675 volumes from the library of the College of Fort William to the Calcutta Public Library. In addition to these books, the donation of books from individuals formed the nucleus of the library. Prince Dwarkanath Tagore was the first proprietor of the Calcutta Public Library. Both the Indian and foreign books, especially from Britain, were purchased for the library. In the report of 1850 we find that the library started collecting books in Gujarati, Marathi, Pali, Ceylonese and Punjabi. The Government of Bengal and North Western Provinces regularly made by individuals as well as donations.

The Calcutta Public Library had a unique position as the first public library in this part of the country. Such a well-organized and efficiently run library was rare even in Europe during the first half of the 19th century. Because of the efforts of the Calcutta Public Library, the National Library has developed rare books and journals in its collection The Imperial Library was formed in 1891 by combining a number of Secretariat libraries. Of these, the most important and interesting was the library of the Home Department, which contained many books formerly belonging to the library of East India College, Fort William and the library of the East India Board in London. But the use of the library was restricted to the superior officers of the Government. Lord Curzon, the then Governor

General of India, was the person who conceived the idea of opening a library for the use of the public. He noticed both the libraries, Imperial Library and Calcutta Public Library, were under-utilized for the want of facilities and he decided to amalgamate the rich collection of both of these libraries. He was successful in effecting the amalgamation of Calcutta Public Library with the then Imperial Library under certain terms.

The library, called Imperial Library, was formally opened to the public on 30th January 1903 at Metcalf Hall, Kolkata. After the independence, the Government of India changed the name of the Imperial Library as the National Library, with an enactment of the Imperial Library (change of name) Act 1948 and the collection was shifted from the Esplanade to the present Belvedere Estate. On 1st February 1953 the National Library opened to the public. The Library is under the Department of Culture, Ministry of Tourism & Culture, and Government of India. The National Library receives deposit of a copy of every publication published in India under Delivery of Books and Newspapers (Public Libraries) Act, 1954. The Central Reference Library started publishing the Indian National Bibliography since 1958. The Government of India appointed a Committee to review the functioning of the national library in 1968. The recommendations of the Committee were accepted for improvement of the national library services. In 1988 a computer division was set up to modernize the operations and services. The digitization and archiving of rare and brittle books were undertaken.

The Language Divisions of the National Library acquire, process and provide reading material in all major Indian languages, namely Assamese (12,000), Bengali (85,000), Gujarati (37,000), Hindi (80,000), Kannada (32,000), Kashmiri (500), Malayalam (34,500), Marathi (37,000), Oriya (19,500), Tamil (57,000) and Urdu (20,000).

2.3.2. Khuda Bakhsh Oriental Public Library, Patna

The Khuda Bakhsh Oriental Public Library, Patna had its origin in the personal collection of a bibliophile, Maulvi Khuda Bakhsh who donated his entire collection of 4000 Oriental manuscripts to the nation by a deed of trust. It was open for the public in October 1891 by Sir Charles Elliot, Governor of Bengal. Acknowledging the immense historical and intellectual value of its rich and valued collection, the Govt. of India declared the Library as Institution of National Importance by an act of Parliament, Kudha Bakhsk Oriental Public Library Act, 1969. The Library is now fully funded by the Ministry of Culture (Govt. of India). This autonomous institution is governed by a Board with the Governor of Bihar as its ex-officio Chairman. The Library has rich collection of Mughal paintings, calligraphy and book decorations, besides manuscripts in Arabic and Urdu languages.

2.3.3. Rampur Raza Library, Rampur (Uttar Pradesh)

Rampur Raza Library, Rampur (Uttar Pradesh) had its origin in the personal collection of Nawab Faizullah Khan who ruled the state of Rampur, from 1774 to 1794. He established the library with his personal modest collection kept in the Tosha Khana of his Palace. The Government of India took over the library on 1 July 1975 under the Act of Parliament and declared it as an institution of national importance. The library is under Department of Culture, Government of India. It contains very rare and valuable collection of manuscripts, historical documents, specimens of Islamic calligraphy, miniature paintings, astronomical instruments and rare illustrated works in Arabic and Persian languages besides 80,000 printed books.

2.3.4. Thanjavur Maharaja Serfoji's Sarasvati Mahal Library, Thanjavur (Tamil Nadu)

Thanjavur Maharaja Serfoji's Sarasvati Mahal

Library, Thanjavur (Tamil Nadu) is one of the oldest libraries existing in the world and possesses very rare and valuable collections of manuscripts, books, maps and paintings on all aspects of Art, Culture and Literature. The library was patronized as Royal Palace Library by the Nayak Kings of Thanjavur (1535-1675 AD) and the Maratha rulers (1676-1855). In 1918 this Library was made as a public Library. Now it is under the possession of the state of Tamil Nadu. In honor of the great royal Marathan patron, King Serfoji, the official name of the library was changed as Thanjavur Maharaja Serfoji's Sarasvati Mahal Library. A body constituted by the Government under a registered society and financed by the Central and State Governments now administers the library.

2.3.5. Prominent Public Libraries in Andhra Pradesh

There are a number of prominent libraries in Andhra Pradesh, which can be considered on par with prominent libraries mentioned above. However, they remained dormant due to lack of patronage and recognition as libraries of national importance. Some of the major libraries are: Srikrishnadevaraya Andhra Basha Nilayam, Sultan Bazar, Hyderabad; Andhra Sarvaswatha Nilayam, Vetapalem; Gowthami Library (now Regional Library), Rajahmundry; Salar Jung Museum Library, Hyderabad; Asafiya Library (now State Central Library), Hyderabad; etc.

2.4. LIBRARY MOVEMENT IN INDIA

As discussed earlier in Section 2.2.3, the credit of establishing libraries for the public goes to Maharaja Sayaji Rao Gaekward (1852-1930) of The Baroda State. W.A. Borden was invited from USA to establish a network of libraries at state, district, taluk and village levels. Thus the library movement in India was initiated. In the more or less same decades, the library movement was spread to the states like Andhra Pradesh, Punjab, West Bengal and Kerala. Library movements are social movements and contributed to the formation of public opinion for the establishment of library system in various states of India.

2.4.1. Library Movement in Andhra Pradesh

The library movement in Andhra Pradesh was a people's movement spread to all regions. The success of public library movement in Andhra Desa can be traced to the beginning of the 19th century. It grew steadily in the subsequent decades. In the year 1800, a private library belonging to Paravasthu Family was declared open for the public. It was subsequently developed as Arsha Grandhalaya. Raja Rameshwar Rayalu's (1821-1865) library was also opened to the public at Wanaparthy and Mahabubnagar. In Rajahmundry, a public library was opened by Justice James Thomas in 1839. The Theosophical Society opened a Library at Guntur in 1850. Mudigonda Sankaradhya promoted the Sankaranda Library in Secunderabad in 1872.

In 1886, Sarswathi nilayam was started by Manthane Adinarayana Murthy, a school teacher. Historically, this library was the first public library ever conceived and started by a single individual in Andhra Desa. In the Telangana region of the former Hyderabad state, a library was established by Mulla Abdul Qayum, a nationalist and a patriot and Moulvi Syed Hussain Bilgrami (Nawab Emadul Mulla), in the year 1886. This was later acquired by the Nizam's Government and declared open to the public. This was named "Asafia Library" and converted in to State Central Library in 1892. Slowly and steadily, libraries and reading clubs sprang up in several parts of Andhra Desa. The following can be mentioned as examples; the Sarswathi Vilasamu at Pulivendula, Cuddapah District (1892); C.V.N. Library, Ongole (1890); the Simhachalapathi Rao Library, Vijayanagaram (1894); the Naoroji Club, Undi (1895); Veeresalingam Kavi

Samajam, Kumundavalli (now in West Godavari District) (1897); Gautami Grandhalayam, Rajahmundary (1898); Vardhamana Samajam, Nellore (1906); the Reading Club, Kolluru(in Guntur District) (1899); the Youngmen's Literary Association, Guntur (1900). During 1907–1908, it led to a growing demand from the people for more libraries and centers of information in different parts of the state. The Ram Mohan Library was established at Vijayawada by Ayyanki Venkata Ramanaiah in 1911, the Andhra Grandhalayam by M. Ramachandra Rao at Kurnool in 1920 and Saraswathi Niketanam by V.V. Shreshti at Vetapalem, in 1911.

In the former state of Hyderabad of which Telangana formed a part, as in the British India, library movement paved the way for and gave strength to political, social and cultural renaissance of the people. Against the peculiar conditions under the Nizam's autocratic rule in Hyderabad state, the library movement helped in forging an awareness and unity among the Telugu people to fight the oppression by feudal force. The rulers wanted to suppress the library movement by issuing the notorious circular (No.53) in 1929, which banned establishment of a library, school or obtaining such permission became a very difficult task.

At the beginning of the 20th century (i.e., 1901) Sri Krishna Devaraya Andhra Bhasha Nilayam was established as a result of the devotion and dynamism of Ravichetti Ranga Rao, the Raja of Munagula. From 1901 onwards, the library movement in the Hyderabad state became a popular movement. It derived its motivation, strength and direction from the people themselves. With the establishment of Sri Krishna Devaraya Andhra Bhasha Nilayam, the library movement gained momentum and libraries were established at several other places in Telangana. Mention may be made of Raja Raja Narendra Andhra Bhasha Nilayam (1904) established in Hanamkonda by the efforts of Madapati Hanumantha Rao, the Andhra Samvardhani (1905) at Secundrabad, Andhra Vijnana Prakashini Grandhna Nilayam (1917) at Suryapet. Sri Vemana Andhra Bhasha Nilayam (1923) at Siddiambar Bazar, Hyderabad. Bala Saraswati, Andhrav Bhasha Nilayam at Afzal Ganj, Hyderabad Prathaparudra Andhra Bhasha Nilayam (1924) at Manikonda; Desodaraka Andhra Bhasha Nilayam (1925) at Kukkunuru and Vijnana Niketanam, (1936) at Khammam. By the year 1925, under the dynamic leadership of Madapati Hanumantha Rao, nearly 100 libraries were established throughout Telangana. Suravaram Pratapa Reddy, another notable personality, through his journalistic activity rendered valuable services for the spread of library movement in the Telangana region.

2.4.2. Aims and Objectives of the Library Movement

The aim of the library movement is to disseminate knowledge among the people and pathetic condition for better living. The old idea that a public library is a mere storehouse of books and the librarian is its custodian only became outdated. The library movement conceived that a public library is a “people’s university”. In the words of S.V. Narasimha Sastri, “its aim is to unfold the varied faculties of every individual comprised in the body politic, man or woman, child or adult, rich or poor, literate or illiterate by adopting appropriate means and methods in each case in accordance with the idiosyncrasies, tastes, environment, intellectual equipment and the like”. The library movement aimed at achieving on overall development of human personality and to realize the objective of the library as an effective means. The movement wished to spread knowledge among the people and thereby awaken the “atma” of the individual steep ignorance and inertia and help him in leading a truthful and purposeful life in society. The Library Movement in Andhra Pradesh ran almost parallel to the national movement and social movement in other parts of the India.

The glorious history of libraries and library movement in Andhra Pradesh can be studied under two broad headings:

- Development of libraries up to 1901 AD
- Development of libraries up to 1960

2.4.3. Development of Libraries upto 1901 A.D.

Andhra Pradesh has a rich tradition of learning. The history of Andhra Pradesh reveals that during the Buddhist period Acharya Nagarjuna established a residential university at Ari Parvath, the Hill abode of Nagarjuna, on the banks of river Krishna in Andhra Pradesh. This library was rich in its collection. Afterwards, a number of libraries were established and managed during 10th, 11th, 15th, 16th, centuries in different parts of the state. However, the success of the public library movement in Andhra Desa can be traced to the beginning of the nineteenth century. The landmarks, in this period, were the establishment of a private library belonging to Paravasthu family which was later developed as Arsha Granthalaya, Likewise, during this period a number of libraries were established, mostly by private efforts. As far as the Telangana region is concerned, private libraries played a dominant role during the nineteenth century.

2.4.4. Development of Libraries upto 1960

In 1901, Sri Krishna Deva Raya Andhra Bhasha Nilayam was established and from then onwards the library movement in the Hyderabad state became a popular movement which derived its motivation, strength and direction from the people themselves. According to Raju (1988), by 1914, there were nearly 163 libraries scattered all over Andhra Desa without any central authority to coordinate their activities or to promote their growth. Another landmark is the organization of the First Andhra Desa Librarians Conference on 10th April, 1914 which led to the establishment of Andhra Desa Granthalaya Sangham. After the establishment of this

Sangham, the library movement gained sufficient momentum in Andhra Desha with the untiring efforts of Sarvashri Ayyanki Venkata Ramanayya, Chilkamarthi Lakshmi Narasimham and Suri Venkata Narasimha Sastry and others. The major activities in the library movement during this period are, Granthalaya yatras otherwise known as library pilgrimages, boat library service, street plays, etc. In the library movement in Andhra Pradesh, the publication of *Granthalaya Sarvasvamu* which was started as a quarterly journal in 1915 is a land mark and currently it is being brought out as monthly journal. The stalwarts in the library movement in the Telangana region were Sarvashri K. Lakshman Rao, Madapati Hanumantha Rao, Suravaram Pratapa Reddy, K.V.Ranga Reddy, T.Ranga Rao, A Veerabhadra Rao, B.Rama Krishna Rao, M.Narsinga Rao and others. Thus, the library movement in Andhra Pradesh during this period helped not only the reading habits, but created a social consciousness among the people. It extended support to various social and political movements in Andhra Pradesh and made people evaluate the importance if public libraries.

The first Public Libraries Act in free India was enacted in the year 1948, named as Madras Public Libraries Act which paved the way for the development of Public Libraries in the ten composite Madras State. This Act was implemented in 1950 onwards in twelve Andhra District which formed part and parcel of the Composite Madras State. Subsequently, in 1955, Hyderabad Public Libraries Act was enacted for implementation in the ten Telangana region. With the states reorganization in the year 1956, the newly formed Government of Andhra Pradesh enacted a fresh act named as Andhra Pradesh Public Libraries Act (1960), which came into effect from 01-04-1960.

2.5. LIBRARY LEGISLATION IN INDIA

Enactment of library legislation gives public libraries

a structure, integrated system of libraries, continuous and definite financial support, qualified personnel, planned organization and growth, permanency and efficiency to libraries. In the absence of legislation, the establishment and maintenance of public libraries will be haphazard. Hence, several seminars, committees and writings of the experts emphasized that the public libraries should be established under the clear mandate of law, so framed as to ensure nation-wide provision of public library service. Legislation aims to ensure proper assessment of library needs, evaluation of existing services and planning of new services, etc. Legislation also provides a system, which can function independently and without being affected by the change in the government and bureaucracy.

2.5.1. Advisory Committee for Libraries on Legislation

The Advisory Committee for Libraries, constituted by the Government of India (1958), proposed certain functions of library legislation. Among which, the major ones include –

1. Legislation should clearly define the government's responsibility in the matter of public libraries;
2. Legislation should lay down the constitution and functions of the library authority at national, state and district level;
3. Legislation should provide and assured basis for library finance;
4. Legislation should lay down the structure of the public library system, and
5. Legislation should provide for participation of the representative of the public in the work of the public libraries at all levels.

The main purpose of a public library is to help a reader to use documents for enriching his knowledge or for leisure time occupation or any other purpose. An effective means of designing and developing a Public Library Service is in the form of a network of a central point linking a number of activities. The type of hierarchy reflects the administrative units for revenue and state administration. The libraries can be organized as tiers in a radical fashion where a state library will have divisional Library. Each Divisional Library becomes the radical focus to the District Library. Each district Library to Branch Library and each Branch Library becomes a focal point to village libraries and so on. Thus the productive organization of a Library networks an administrative structure. Library Legislation is perhaps the best and assured way of providing Library Services in a democratic and free society. Basing on the experience of drafting the first Model Library Act of Dr. S.R. Ranganathan in 1930 the Library Acts which came later have taken above aspects into consideration and have been drafted.

2.5.2. UNESCO Guidelines on Legislation

The UNESCO, as a part of implementing the National Information System (NATIS), also prepared the necessary guidelines on Library Legislation. A legislative framework for implementing the NATIS was drafted by Philip Sewell, A.W. Mabbs and E.M. Broome. The guidelines of the draft are summarized as below:

- Public Library Systems are a key element in NATIS and should have prime consideration when Legislation is being considered.
- A Legislation base is essential for the development of Library systems.
- Legislation should make it mandatory to provide Library Services, but it should be capable of flexible and progressive implementation. The means should be willed as well as the ends.
- There is a need for a national focus with clearly defined responsibilities and powers.

- The nature of the national focus will vary, but will balance in varying degrees the two main forms of organizational structures centralized and decentralized.
- Library service must be equipped with controlling and / or advisory bodies which ensure they are responsive to democratic control and user interests. It was stated in the guidelines that a Public Library Service is essential for the enlightenment of the public and on efficient Library Service is only possible with Library Legislation.

2.5.3. Essential Features of Legislation

The Legislation needs special features like preliminaries, administrative authorities at state level and district level, and equally important are the financial resources and the accountability.

Preliminaries : The Preliminaries constitute the title, authority for Legislation, extent for which it is applicable and the date of implementation of the Act, and the most important are the preamble and the terminology. The Preamble should clearly spell out the objectives of Library Legislation and it should be precise and explicit. The preamble of the world's First Library Act i.e., British Public Libraries Act of 1850 is a torch bearer is those days which pronounces the "founding, maintaining and administering free libraries for the British people, by an permanent rate, equally levied and responsibility expended". In the Danish Act "The purpose of Public Libraries is to promote the spread of knowledge, education and culture by making books and other suitable materials free of charge". The purpose of this Act is to foster and promote the establishment and operation of multi country free Public Libraries service throughout the state in order to give to all of its citizen's equal opportunity of access to comprehensive Library Collections".

Five Functions of Library Legislation : Advisory Committee for Libraries Constituted by the Government of India (1958) proposes the following five functions of Library Legislation:

- It should clearly define the government's responsibilities in the matter of Public Libraries
- Legislation should lay down the Constitution and functions of the Library Authority as national, state and district Levels.
- Legislation should provide an assured basis for Library Finance. There are two ways of providing a firm basis for Library Finance:
  - (i) A special Library cess; and
  - (ii) Reservation of a certain percentage of the education budget.
- Legislation should lay down the structure of the Public Library System.
- Legislation should provide for participation of the representative of the public, in the work of the Public Libraries at all levels.

Factors of Library Legislation : The Public Libraries Section of the International Federation of Library Associations & Institutions (IFLA) prepared a working paper on the "Development of Public Library Services" in which one section was devoted to Public Library Legislation. The recommendations are listed below:

- Appropriate local authorities must be empowered to expend public funds for Public Library purposes.
- The amount of expenditure should not be limited.
- The public library proposes funds to be expended shall be so defined as not to restrict development.
- Local authorities should be empowered to enter into arrangements with other authorities for joint schemes for providing the whole or any part of the service.

- Each local authority should appoint a Library Committee directly which will be responsible to the local council. The Librarian should have the right to attend all meetings of the Librarian Committee.
- Each local authority should have the power to appoint staff who shall be employed in accordance with the conditions and regulations applicable with suitable variations to other local government officers.
- The use of all services provided must be made available to all the in habitants free.
- Through each local authority provides services primarily for the use of its own inhabitants and those who work or study in its area and other persons, living outsides that area, should be able to use, those services if they wish.
- As soon as practicable, all appropriate local authorities should be legally obliged to maintain adequate public library services.
- All public Librarians should provide users with "Open Access" to adequate stocks of books for reference and borrowing.
- Library staff must be recruited from persons with a good general education and must be professionally qualified.
- Library staff must be adequately remunerated.
- Scales of salaries should provide for the varying degrees of responsibility, specialization and experience involved in the several positions found on the establishment of library system of different sizes and types; and adequate opportunities for promotion and personal growth and advancement must exist.
- The number of staff employed by each authority must be sufficient to permit all necessary duties to be carried out completely and satisfactorily.

- Schools of library science must be maintained.
- The existence of a well organized Library association is essential, where the above requirements are not met, the service for the public as a whole suffers gravely.
- Probably the most important factor in determining the state of Library development is the way in which the functions of public libraries are understood by Librarians and authorities and by the public itself. If the concept of the service to civilized and progressive community is accepted, it will be supported by all men and of good will.

Principles of Library Legislation

The major principles of public library legislation are as follows:

- The Library Legislation must be simple and general. It should be flexible allowing the future development of libraries.
- It must be kept above political changes.
- The law should create conditions which are helpful for the development of libraries.
- It should state the duties and privileges of public libraries. The terms of financial assistance must also be mentioned. The law also must recognize the existence of other types of libraries in the country.
- With regard to public libraries, the law should also specify the responsibilities of local, state and central Governments.
- The law also should provide recommendations for the establishment of librarians by the State Governments or prescribe how grants will be made available if they are run by the local governments.
- The law must prescribe that Public Libraries are free to all categories of people by providing necessary resources.

- All Librarians must lend their books free of charge to all citizens in the country
- The books in the Library should reflect all shades of opinion, that is to say, no censorship should be imposed. The Library should be at liberty to buy any books that are needed by the user.
- The Legislation should also make provisions for the creation of an advisory body at the state or National level.
- Legislation should also provide deposit and participation and in national and international co – operation.
- Legislation should also make provision for sufficient documentation and bibliographical services.
- Provisions should be made for the training of Librarians.

Library Legislation provides the necessary mandate, direction and finances for the development of Public Libraries. Library Legislation is supposed to give the public libraries better prospects of stability, development and required finances. In the absence of mandate, the finances provided for the public libraries were left to the vagaries of governments without any definite commitment. In order to put public libraries on a proper track there is a need for legislation that would solve many library problems. Moreover, it is a well accepted principle that in all the civilized societies it is the responsibility of the government to provide adequate library and information services to its citizens both urban and rural areas. Public libraries are supposed to be people's universities. Hence, the expenditure on public libraries should aim at fixing the financial responsibilities upon the government in connection with the library staff, reading materials, building, furniture, equipment, etc.

2.5.4. Dr. S. R. Ranganathan and Public Library Legislation

The privilege of proposing the Model Public Library Bill (1930) and struggle for enactment of the first public library act in India in 1948 goes to none other than the doyen of library science in India, Dr. S.R. Ranganathan. The occasion for drafting the first Model Libraries Act came only in 1930, while Dr S.R. Ranganathan was engaged in writing his well known classic "Five Laws of Library Science". In that book second law "Every reader his/her book" stresses the need for legislation. At the same time Prof. P. Seshadri of Banaras Hindu University asked him to be the secretary of the Library Service Section of the "First All Asia Educational Conference", which was held in Banaras in 1930. This provided an opportunity to have the Draft Model Act discussed at the conference. This Model Act is the seed out of which Library Legislation grew in India. Dr. S R Ranganathan strived a lot for library legislation and prepared different library bills for the Indian Union and constituent states, such as Model Library Act for constituent states of India (1930); Bengal (1931); Bombay (1946); Central Province and Berar (1946); Old Madras state (1946) which later became Act in 1948; United Province (1947); Cochin (1947); Travancore (1947); Union Government (1948); Madhya Pradesh (1950); Union and Constituent States (1950); Constituent States (1957); Union (1957); West Bengal (1958); Kerala (1959); Uttar Pradesh (1960); Mysore (1961) which became Act in 1965; Assam (1964); Gujarat (1964 and Model Library Bill (1972).

2.5.5. Model Public Library Bills

There are Five Model Library Bills proposed by eminent persons, working groups or committees, namely, Dr. S.R. Ranganathan (1930, revised in 1972), Sen Committee (1963), Working Group of the Planning Commission (1964), Dr. Velaga Venkatappaiah (1989, 1995). With some variation, like finance (cess or grants), constitution of committee, etc., most of the Acts have their base in the Model Library Act of Dr. S.R. Ranganathan.

1. Model Public Libraries Act of Dr. S. R. Ranganathan : As described earlier, the first Model Public Libraries Act was prepared by Dr. S R Ranganathan in 1930 and revised in 1957 and 1972. It was discussed at the First All Asia Educational Conference held at Banaras during 26-30 December 1930. It was introduced in West Bengal Legislature in 1931 and in Madras Legislature in 1933. The Bill could not be passed due to financial clauses on library grant, library cess etc. The salient features of final version are:

- Establishment of public libraries in city, rural and other areas;
- Constitution of State Library Authority i.e. Minister of Education;
- Constitution of State Library Committee as an advisory body of the State Library Authority;
- Constitution of Local Library Authority for each city and one for each district;
- State Library Authority, Government and Local Library Authority may determine library rate in such a manner and may determine collection of library cess from time to time.

2. Model Public Libraries Bill of Ministry of Education : The Government of India, Ministry of Education appointed an Advisory Committee for Libraries in 1957, under the Chairmanship of Shri K P Sinha, former Director of Public Instruction, Bihar. This committee recommended the need for library legislation for each state. As a follow-up action of the Advisory Committee, the Ministry of Education, Government of India appointed a committee under the Chairmanship of Dr. M D Sen. The Committee drafted Model Public Libraries Bill in the year 1963. The salient components of this Bill are:

- Constitution of State Library Authority as an apex body to advise the Government in the matter of library developments;
- Constitution of State Library Directorate for direction and controlling of library services;
- Constitution of District Library Committee in each district;
- Treatment of employees as government servant;
- Collection of library cess at the rate of 6 paisa per rupee on house tax and property tax.

3. Model Public Libraries Bill of the Planning Commission : The Planning Commission, Government of India, constituted a 'Working Group on Libraries' in 1964 to plan and advice on the development of Libraries during the Fourth Five Year Plan. The Working Group recommended a Library Development Scheme to be implemented during the Fourth Plan period with a financial commitment of Rs.309 million, which was appended by Model Public Libraries Bill and submitted its report in 1965. Bill was not considered even by a single state. The Bill included the following features:

- Establish, maintain, develop and integrated adequate public library service in the state;
- Constitution of Committee of Experts to prescribe the standards of service;
- Constitution of State Library Council to advise the government for the promotion and development of library service;
- Establishment of State Library Directorate to control, direct and supervise library system in the state;
- Establishment of State Central Library, State Regional Libraries and District Libraries;
- Treatment of employees in the system of State Government Servants

- Government shall be the financial source and shall maintain the public library system in the state

4. Model Public Libraries Bill of Indian Library Association : The Indian Library Association (ILA) formed in 1933, has keen interest in library legislation. The ILA discussed library legislation at its various seminars organized in 1964, 1978 and 1981. Consequently, ILA Council at its meeting held on 23 June 1989, keeping in view of the developments and experiences gain from the existing Acts, resolved to prepare a Modelm Library Bill. Accordingly, as asked by ILA, Dr. Velaga Venkatappaiah, Chairman, Central

Sectional Committee on Public Libraries of the ILA prepared a Model Public Library Bill. ILA accepted the draft Bill with minor changes at its National Seminar on Public Library Legislation in 1990 at the final product of the Model Public Libraries Bill was published in 1991. The Bill was circulated to all the states and union territories but few states reacted favorably to the Bill. This Model Bill was again discussed in a National Seminar on Library Legislation and revised as the Model State Public Library and Information Service Act in 1995. In view of emergence of Information Technology at all levels, the model act was again revised in 2000. The important components of this Bill are:

- State Library and Information Service, based on a State Policy;
- Constitution of State Library Authority at the apex level with Minister of Libraries as Chairman as policy making and executive body;
- Establishment of Directorate of Public Libraries for directing, controlling and supervising;
- Constitution of City, District Library Authority for rendering service from district to village level;
- Provision for network of Public Library and Information Services from state to village level;

- Constitution of State Library and Information Service;
- Collection of Library cess on house tax and property tax, entertainment tax, professional tax, vehicle tax, etc.;
- Constitution of State Boards for education, book production, co-ordination, etc.;
- Accountability of public expenditure and services.

5. Model Union Library Act : The Government of India appointed a committee to explore the possibilities to establish a National Central Library at New Delhi in 1948. Dr. S R Ranganathan, a member of the committee drafted a Library Development plan in 1950 with a 30-year programme and a draft Library Bill for the states and Union Public Library Act. This was revised in 1959 and again in 1972. However, libraries falls under the state list of the constitution and it may not be possible to pass Bill as a Union Act, unless and until the constitution is suitably amended for this purpose. The main features of this model Act are:

- Constitution of a National Library Authority;
- Establishment of national central libraries;
- Constitution of National Library Committee as an advisory body
- to the National library Authority;
- Constitution of National library fund;
- Amendment to the delivery of Books and Newspaper Act, 1954.

2.4.6. States with Public Library Legislation

During the last six decades, 14 (fourteen) Public Library Bills were enacted in different states of India, such as:

1. Tamil Nadu : The Tamil Nadu (Madras) Public Libraries Act 1948;

2. Andhra Pradesh : The Andhra Pradesh Public Libraries Act 1960; (previously known as The Hyderabad Public Libraries Act 1955, but renamed as a result of State Reorganization);

3. Karnataka : The Karnataka (Mysore) Public Libraries Act 1965;

4. Maharashtra : The Maharastra Public Libraries Act 1967. (The Kolhapur Public Libraries Act was passed in 1945. Consequent upon the state reorganization, the state of Kolhapur was merged with Maharashtra state. Then Maharashtra Public Libraries Act came into being in 1967);

5. West Bengal : The West Bengal Public Libraries Act 1979;

6. Manipur : The Manipur Public Libraries Act 1988;

7. Kerala : The Kerala Public Libraries Act 1989;

8. Haryana : The Haryana Public Libraries Act 1989;

9. Mizoram : The Mizoram Public Libraries Act 1993;

10. Goa : The Goa Public Libraries Act 1993;

11. Orissa : Orissa Public Libraries Act, 2001;

12. Gujarat : Gujarat Public Libraries Act, 2001;

13. Uttaranchal : Uttaranchal Public Libraries Act, 2005.

14. Rajasthan : Rajasthan Public Libraries Act, 2006

15. Uttar Pradesh Public Libraries Act, 2006.

16. Pondicherry Public Libraries Act, 2007.

17. Bihar Public Libraries Act, 2007.

18. Chhattisgarh Public Libraries Act, 2007.

19. Arunachal Pradesh Public Libraries Act, 2009.

2.6. PUBLIC LIBRARY ACTS OF DIFFERENT STATES IN INDIA

The following table provides a picture of essential features of the library acts in 14 states of India:

Essential Features

- Out of 28 states in India, only 14 states have enacted public library legislation after Independence. The oldest public library act was Madras Public Libraries Act, 1948 and the latest one was Rajasthan Public Libraries Act, 2006. No Union Territory has passed public library legislation so far.
- The apex body of the public library system at the state level is State Library Committee / Council / Authority, which is advisory in nature in all states; however, in few states it also acts as authority. In Andhra Pradesh the apex body is Granthalaya Parishad, a nominated body of the State Government.
- Director of Public Libraries is the head of the public library system in almost all states in India, who administers the public library system in their respective states.
- At the district level, district library authority/ council/committee is responsible for supervision and management of libraries. In Andhra Pradesh, it is Zilla Granthalaya Samstha. The chairman of district library authority is either nominated (in some states like Andhra Pradesh) or elected. In West Bengal, the District Magistrate acts as a ex-officio chairman for District Library authority.
- The employees of the public libraries in Tamil Nadu, Karnataka, Maharastra, West Bengal, Manipur and Kerala are government servants. In Andhra Pradesh, the Secretary of Zilla Granthalaya Samstha is government servants, while others are on par with local bodies. In some acts it is not clearly mentioned.
- Library cess is the main source of revenue in states like Tamil Nadu, Andhra Pradesh, Karnataka and Kerala. In the acts, most of which came later opted for grants from governments rather library cess.

2.7. THE STATE CENTRAL LIBRARY

One of the most important provisions made by the Library Acts in India is the creation of an Apex Public Library in each state. This apex library is called by different Public Library Acts either as "State Central Library", or "State Library" and it is supposed to assume a leadership role to guide all the public libraries in the state. According to the ALA *Glossary* (1983), a State Central Library is defined as "a library maintained by state funds for the use of state officials and employees, and usually for the use of all citizens of the state". It is a public library for the use of the citizens. As it is created by the state governments in their respective state headquarters and acts as an apex library of the public library systems in the concerned state it is called as State Central Library. There are a total of 30 such libraries in different states and union territories of India. Excluding Pondicherry (Union Territory), the four states in south India have well established State Central Libraries, which were well supported by the public library acts of their respective states.

The Andhra Pradesh Public Libraries Act (1960) simply states that State Central Library means 'a library established by the Government as the State Central Library'. Ekbote Committee, which was appointed by the Government of Andhra Pradesh, to review the functioning of APPL Act (1978), regretted that the lending section and the reading room dominate the library service relegating the reference and research work of the library to the background. The Committee enumerated the following main functions need to be performed by the State Central Library:

- To collect all literary scientific technological and other materials produced in the state both current and historical. It would include the copyright collection of books published within the state.
- To be the main source in the state of reference materials for scholars and research workers.

- To act as an authority for the compilation of the state bibliography of all the books, periodicals, newspapers, and other reading materials in the state.
- To serve as the focal point and organizing agency for inter – regional, inter – state loans of books and the other library materials. It should be the centre of inter – library co –operation.
- To act as a clearing house of information on all state and national matters including commercial, industrial, technical and others information asked for by any library in the state or by anyone else.,
- To organize book exhibition and professional and library conferences.
- To make provision for in – service training of librarians.

The Committee also made 19 recommendations on various aspects to improve the services of the state central library. Some of them have been considered, yet many of them still to be implemented. An in depth study of all the model library bills and the library acts of various states in south India is necessary to understand the various provisions with regard to state central library and to examine their implementation critically and analytically. Their relevance in the present technological environment is also need to be thoroughly examined.

Taher, Mohamed (1997) opines, "If the state central library should function as an apex library both in becoming a repository (of all the documents and published material) and a lending reference library, the most fundamental thing is overhauling the entire library system – staff, resources, attitudes, motivation, and finance. The legislation needs to be amended to adopt these basic roles (repository and reference). If the repository function requires national copyright act changes and hence consumes time, it is worth to change the SCL immediately as a `State Central Reference Library'. The observation is equally applicable to State Central Libraries of all four southern states of India.

The prominent public libraries at the national and state level did not spring up through legislation; however, they received continuous financial support and authority as public institutions for the equal service to every member in the society. Though many attempts were made to cover all states of entire country, only 14 states could enact public library legislation. The four states of South India, namely, Tamil Nadu, Andhra Pradesh, Karnataka and Kerala, were in the forefront to adopt public library legislation in the country. Being at the apex of the public library system of their respective states the State Central Libraries need to assume leadership role. However, the criticism from the professionals indicates that the organization of resources and delivery of services are not satisfactory. Therefore, an in-depth study is needed.

REFERENCES

1. ALA Glossary of Library Terms (1983). Chicago: ALA
2. Andhra Pradesh (1978). Committee to review the working of the Andhra Public Library Act, 1960 and to suggest amendments to the Act. *Report.* Hyderabad: Govt of A.P. Andhra Pradesh Public Library (Amendment) Act (1989). Hyderabad: Govt of A.P. Danish Act.
3. Ekbote, Gopal Rao (1987). *Public library system.* Hyderabad: Ekbote Brothers. India. Advisory Committee for Libraries (1959). *Report.* Delhi: Manager of Publications. India. Ministry of Human Resource Development (1986). *Report of Committee on National Policy on Library and Information System.* New Delhi: MHRD.
4. Khuda Bakhsh Oriental Library *http://kblibrary.bih.nic.in*
5. National Library of India. *http://www.nationallibrary.gov.in*
6. Raju, A.A.N. (1988). *Library Movement in Andhra Pradesh.* Delhi: Ajanta Publications.
7. Ramaiah, L.S. and Sankara Reddy, M. (2010). Position and status of public libraries in India: Acritical study. In *National*

conference on public libraries in the knowledge societies/ edited by L.S. Ramaiah et al. Vijayawada: APLA., p.9-19.

8. Rampur Raza Library *http://razalibrary.gov.in*
9. Ranganathan, S.R. (1953). *Library legislation: Handbook to Madras Library Act.* Madras: MALA.
10. Taher, Mohamed (1997). Functions of the state central libraries: A case study of A.P. Staten Central Library, Hyderabad. In *Public library services: system and networking/* edited by LS Ramaiah et al. New Delhi: Ess Ess. Vol.2; p.23.
11. UNESCO. *Guidelines on library legislation* / National Information System drafted by Philip Sewell, A.W. Mabbas and E.M. Broom.
12. Venkatappaiah, V (1982). *Public library system in Andhra Pradesh.* Waltair: Andhra University.
13. Venkatappaiah, V (1990). *Indian library legislation.* 2v. New Delhi: Daya.

3

Information Resources and Services

3.1. DATA, CAPTA AND INFORMATION

Classically, in introductory texts on Information Systems, information is considered to be the output from an information system, with data (raw, unprocessed, collected "facts") being input. This is a very simplistic view and is often qualified by saying that the information only becomes useful if it is in context and is meaningful.

I. Definitions of Data

"**Data** : A representation of facts, concepts or instructions in a formalized manner suitable for communication, interpretation, or processing by humans or by automatic means." (Hicks [1993: 668] quoted by Checkland and Holwell [1998]).

Three aspects of data can be identified. These correspond with the three ontologism, realism, nominalism and socially constructed reality and the corresponding beliefs about physical and social reality (objective, subjective or inter-subjective). As a result they emphasis the different possible roles of data, namely, to:

- Record objective facts which will be understood in exactly the same way by everyone;
- Record absolutely any type of concept, with no guarantees as to its accuracy or validity, which will be interpreted in all sorts of different ways by individuals;
- Use agreed structures and conventions for representing information, recording it and transmitting it, all in order to communicate it.

The objective view tends to assume that all data processing will be automated. The subjective view is very different in that it emphasizes that if data are processed using a computer, the output is still only more highly structured or reformatted data. The inter-subjective view allows for the possibility that data may be processed either by computer or directly by a person.

The objective view makes the following assumptions about data.

- They are factual, resulting from recording of measurable events, or objects.
- They record particular instances of reality.
- Introna [1992: 2.42] takes a purely objective view of data, proclaiming them to be "Aperspectual, ahistorical, acontextual".
- They are explicit as they are in a fixed, recorded form.
- Hence, they can be communicated digitally.
- Modern society generates enormous amounts of data that record details of individual events and objects.
- This objective point of view accepts that the data are validated in the sense that they must be

measured and recorded accurately.

Certain logic checks as to the reasonableness of the data can be done to try to determine whether the data capturing instruments or processes have failed. Data can be shown to be true if they correspond to reality.

The definitions that follow are examples of those that refer only to the objective characteristics of data:

> *"Data represent unstructured facts." (Avison and Fitzgerald [1995: 12] quoted by Checkland and Holwell [1998])*
>
> *"Data: Facts collected from observations or recordings about events, objects or people." (Clare and Loucopoulos [1987: 2] quoted by Checkland and Holwell [1998])*
>
> *"Data: The raw material of organizational life; it consists of disconnected numbers, words, symbols and syllables relating to the events and processes of the business."*

The subjective point of view of data

On the other hand the subjective view makes the following assumptions about data.

- The data are not necessarily true or accurate as not all errors can be detected automatically and not everyone will necessarily agree that they are a true representation of a particular fact.
- Some data record subjective opinion, not facts. If data can represent opinions and concepts, they are not truly objective.
- Data represent information and are the only way we can make information explicit.
- Nothing but data can be communicated digitally or in any other way. Only data are transmitted, be it by means of a telecommunications medium, in printed form, or directly without using any technology.

- Data have absolutely no meaning. They acquire meaning only when appropriated by a human recipient.

The definitions that follow are examples of those that include subjective aspects. These definitions include characteristics which have been highlighted as being objective or inter-subjective as well.

> *"Data: Natural language: facts given, from which others may be deduced, inferred. Information Processing and computer science: signs or symbols, especially for transmission in communication systems and for processing in computer systems, usually but not always representing information, agreed facts or assumed knowledge; and represented using agreed characters, codes, syntax and structure." (Maddison [1989: 168] quoted by Checkland and Holwell [1998])*

> *"By themselves, data are meaningless; they must be changed into a usable form and placed in a context to have value. Data becomes information when they are transformed to communicate meaning or knowledge, ideas or conclusions." (Senn [1982: 62] quoted by Introna [1992]).*

The inter-subjective point of view

- The inter-subjective point of view.
- The purpose of data is to permit communication.
- Information exists before data. Some version of that information can be retrieved from the data.
- Data must be recorded in a formalized structure and knowledge of this structure must be shared as prior shared meaning. They cannot be totally unstructured or no-one would ever be able to process them, but they can be reorganized into more complex

structures during subsequent processing. The structure will result from language syntax and semantics if the data are in the form of text, or in the case of numeric or symbolic data, will depend on the predesigned layout of database records, forms or even the position of the data on a physical object. (We know something about what a number plate denotes from its position on a car even if the format is unfamiliar.)

- They are represented using agreed characters, codes, syntax and structure. A predetermined, agreed way of coding and decoding must be associated with this representation. A stream of bits is not data unless someone has the key by means of which it can be decoded.
- The fact that data are both recorded and have some structure makes them potentially useful - they are in a form suitable for subsequent interpretation and processing. Other information can be inferred and deduced from them and they can be associated with other data. They have potential meaning.
- They have an implied context and history. If the data have been captured or a procedure exists to capture them, a purpose has already been recognized.

Example definitions

"Data: Facts, concepts or derivatives in a form that can be communicated and interpreted." (Galland, [1982: 57] quoted by Checkland and Holwell [1998])

"Data are formalized representations of information, making it possible to process or communicate that information." [Dahlbom & Mathiassen, 1995: 26]

II. Definition of capta

In Checkland and Holwell's terms [1998] the objective facts are data before they are captured but capta once they have been captured as part of an information system or even in interpersonal communication. Hence, what is generally considered to be data, the input to a computer program, is not data but capta as it has a specified format, has a purpose, is meaningful to the program and has context. The data are thus the vast numbers of objective facts that exist in the universe and that could be measured and be collected. The capta are those that have already been identified as worth collecting and for which a form of representation has been chosen. The process of selecting capta from the data is a mental one and may be done subconsciously. This process is generally simply a matter choosing to pay attention to particular facts. Capta are richer than data as they are recognized as relevant (which implies that they are in a context). The fact that context and potential or actual meaning adds to the richness of data is included in many of the definitions of information found in introductory texts for Information Systems students, for example, Lay, Eccles, Julyan and Boot - The principles of business computing Fourth edition [1993:535] and Avison and Fitzgerald [1995:12] quoted by Checkland and Holwell [1998].

Unstructured text such as is found in e-mail and newspapers may be closer to Checkland and Holwell's concept of data, as it is left to the processor (that is, the human reader or receiver) to decide what to use and how. Processing is not specified or automated.

Those data which an individual (or system) considers to be of interest and hence pays attention to are selected and become capta. However, Checkland and Holwell say that processing may be more complex and the data may be classified, that is, associated with other data [1998: 89]. There is, however, some ambiguity in this regard as this is subsequently described as meaning attribution and occurs when capta becomes information.

III. Definitions of information

Definitions of information depend on the way in which the term "data" is defined. The major point of difference is whether information can be produced by an automated process and how this information, which is also digital, recorded and can be transmitted, differs from data.

The objective point of view

- Information is output from a computer program.
- The systems analyst decides what output will be useful. This output remains useful and meaningful regardless who the recipient is.
- The processing which produces the information includes summarizing in order to reduce the volume of data.
- Data may be associated with other data, which may be obtained from different sources, to produce the information.
- The processing (classifying, linking, summarizing, sorting, presentation) adds value in the form of potential meaning. The less structured data are less useful and less meaningful than the more structured information.

In the definition that follows "a meaning" seems to imply that the meaning is fixed and not open to interpretation and, therefore, this definition refers only to the objective characteristics of information:

> *"Information has a meaning ... (it) comes from selecting data, summarizing it and presenting it in such a way that it is useful to the recipient." (Avison and Fitzgerald [1995: 12] quoted by Checkland and Holwell [1998])*

The subjective point of view

- Data become information only once they have been appropriated by the human recipient. Hence, the output from any computer program is still data.
- The added value of information (compared with data) results from the recipient appropriating the new data, interpreting them and placing them in context by combining them with existing personal information.
- Some authors consider data to be information only if they are used by the recipient in making a decision.
- Data become information only if they include something previously unknown to the recipient.
- Introna considers information to be historical, contextual and perspectual [Introna, 1992: 2.42]. It is molded by the life experience (erlebnis) to provide understanding.

The definitions that follow are examples of those that include subjective aspects. These definitions also include some characteristics which are considered to be objective or inter-subjective.

> *"Information usually implies data that is organized and meaningful to the person receiving it. Data is therefore raw material that is transformed into information by data processing. Information can be defined in terms of its surprise value. It tells the recipient something he did not know." (Davis et al [1985: 30] quoted by Introna [1992])*

> *"Information: (1) Data that has been transformed into a meaningful and useful form for specific human beings. (2) The meaning that a human assigns to data by means of the known conventions used in its representations." [Lay et al, 1993: 535]*

"Information is that which results when some human mental activity (observation, analysis) is successfully applied to data to reveal its meaning or significance." (Galland [1982: 127] quoted by Checkland and Holwell [1998]).

"Information is the particular instances of reality as experience, perceived or understood by an individual in a specific context." [Introna, 1992:2.37] "...information comes into being as the receiver appropriates the data and gives it meaning" [Introna, 1992: 2.39].

The inter-subjective point of view

- Aspects of shared meaning and discourse (validity claims [Braaten, 1991: 14]) are characteristic of this point of view.
- The recipient has participated in the systems analysis and hence has influenced the process and has said what output was likely to be meaningful to him and others using the system.
- More advanced, database-oriented, systems allow the user to formulate queries and interact directly with the data in the database. Hence, there is a more dynamic process where the user's judgment is combined with the power of the technology.
- Information "has meaning" which can be communicated versus "is meaning" in the objective point of view.
- Information must be put into some context "... in order to understand something, we already need a preliminary understanding of it" [Dahlbom & Mathiassen, 1995: 32].

This preliminary understanding must be shared in order for a new shared understanding to result.

Preconceptions plus information = interpretation => knowledge

"To produce information we have to interpret what we experience and make explicit what we know." [Dahlbom & Mathiassen, 1995: 26]

IV. Discussion

There are a number of levels of information which are used in different ways and carry different kinds of meaning. The fact that, these are all commonly referred to as information can be confusing.

Information 1 - lean information

The first sort of information is data (or capta) which has been processed electronically (summarized, sorted, classified, analyzed or simply collated and associated with other appropriate data), reformatted and made available to someone who is expected to find it meaningful and useful (and may act on it). The processing associated with the production of this type of information is mechanistic and procedural and can be described by an algorithm. The processing is done deliberately in order to add value. Since this processing was not done by a person, in Checkland and Holwell's terms [1998] this is still capta. In Habermas' terms this type of information is the manifestation of functional rationality (administrative systems). The intention is, therefore, that:

- The information will be used to initiate action or decisions within a clearly delimited scope of function and time, or should be available when action and decisions are required. Its purpose is unambiguous.
- Hence, it generally has a short useful life.
- It has a limited readership for whom it is meaningful and who are authorized to access it. The person who creates the specification of the program that will produce this type of information, specifically intends to produce information that the reader will react to and has a relatively stringently defined target group

in mind who is expected to be very familiar with the context and share the frame-of-reference.

- The information is necessary either because it is not already available or to reduce uncertainty by confirming facts.

Provided that the context is explained, this information is not ambiguous. For example, the trade deficit may be given in a recognized format, for a specified currency, for a specified country, on a certain date, calculated according to a procedure for which a description and explanation are available. • It is specific, not universal, and hence acontextual, ahistorical and not perspectual leading to local knowledge (functional rationality) rather than wisdom or universal knowledge (theoretical rationality).

Information 2 - rich information

What then is the type of information that is not the output from a computer process, such as information in newspapers and text books - text which is intended to inform? Is the difference between Information Systems and Information Science which of these two types of information the subject tries to make available or accessible? This 'information' has been carefully put in context (explained) and a human has done this processing but it is in artifact form (the information is printed on paper or displayed on a computer screen) and is a commodity. In Checkland and Holwell's terms this is still capta, as it is external to the human mind. In Habermas' terms, the intentional behaviour which produces this type of 'information' may be strategic or communicative action and the communicative rationality would be authentic self-expression referring to the aesthetic sphere. It might be instrumental if it consists largely of instructions such as a manual or recipe book. This type of information, which will be called Information, has the following characteristics in comparison with Information1 .

- It is not as likely to initiate immediate actions or decisions as Information1 but is intended to initiate thought and to influence the reader by altering his life world.
- It is produced deliberately for a purpose but this purpose has less well-defined scope and the expected outcomes are less specific.
- It has a wider readership. (The newspaper is not prepared for one specific reader, it is prepared with the intention to inform.)
- It is relevant for a longer period.
- It is less structured than information produced by a computer and has more complete sentences and fewer tables.
- It handles more of the type of information which is "soft" and cannot easily be expressed in terms that are exact or precise. Hence, readers need to interpret the information to a greater extent than the first type.

It is for this reason that it is likely to contain more redundant information and that the context is usually explained in greater detail - except where it is assumed that the context is already known, in which case the information may be very difficult for "an outsider" to understand. It handles more complex information, where more explanation is required. (Although this might not be considered to be discourse because it is not interactive or a dialogue, it can certainly present one or more sides of an argument and try, by force of the better argument, to convince the reader of a particular "truth".)

- It is sometimes specific but may also attempt to explain universal "truths".
- It is perceptual in the sense that most complex information, formulated by a person, includes that person's perspective, slant, or bias.

The two types of information are related: Both are intended to present facts (and in the case of Information2, may include opinions) in a form which will probably (hopefully) communicate meaning to the recipient. In Information1 ambiguity is avoided. In Information2 ambiguity may be inevitable and is sometimes courted. Information1 is "lean". Information2 is "rich". The more subtle and equivocal a text is, the richer it may be considered to be. It is easier to refer to both lean and rich information as information even before it is appropriated and hence, for the moment, neither Introna's nor Checkland and Holwell's terminology is used. Both Information1 and Information2 are processed data in a sense. In the one case, a computer has done predetermined calculations and processing to produce the information. In the second case, a person has either intuitively or deliberately processed the information and combined it with his or her unique world view, possibly analysed, synthesised or evaluated it but definitely expressed it in an individual way. As with all aspects of technology, appropriate fit between the task and the technology is important although it is not the only factor involved in adopting a specific technology. Rich information corresponds largely with "thick information". "In fact in one area - so called thick information - management technology can be dangerously limiting. As defined by Henry Mintzberg of McGill University, thick information is irrational, subjective, intuitive knowledge that transcends what can be categorized on an MIS report." [Davidow & Malone, 1992: 170]

Information 3 - appropriated information

When a human acquires information and mentally processes it, some form of learning occurs. The user or acquirer of information relates it to existing knowledge and information and a third type of information results. During this process meaning is attributed to the information. It is possible to assimilate isolated facts but it is easier to remember information that can be related to an existing mental landscape (or a world view, or mental model). Information3 is personal and mentally stored and has meaning. This is the richest information. It is impossible to express it exactly and completely. Hence Information3 cannot be transferred. It may change from day to day. It probably does not correspond entirely with anyone else's version. How it is structured is unknown. The creation of Information3 is the process of learning. Further learning can occur without further input of Information2, as the learner restructures the information and associates it with other personal beliefs, values and knowledge. This is the 'true information' according to Checkland and Holwell [1998] and Introna [1992]. Introna [1992] explains the process of developing understanding in terms of the hermeneutic circle. Interpretations of text follow a cycle in which a new element is interpreted alone and then in terms of the larger text. This results in a re-interpretation of the meaning of the text as a whole. The new element may then be re-interpreted in terms of the new understanding of the complete text. Thus, the individual starts off with certain prior knowledge or prejudices in order to form an initial understanding of a text. This new information is then related to the larger context of the learner's life world (traditions, economic and social situation) and he arrives at a new understanding of the life world. New understanding now influences the more particular interpretation of the text and this will be modified. Once again the modified information will be related to the broader context, and once again this might be adjusted to reach a consistent view. This process will continue until the new information and the larger picture no longer have any inconsistencies.

Information - tacit information

Certain types of information are more difficult than

others to put into words. Tacit information may be difficult to verbalize. In fact some skills, such as balancing while riding a bicycle, do not seem to have words that describe them. Hence, this information is usually imparted by demonstrating it and by the recipient learning by trial and error or practicing the skill.

Another type of interpersonal communication that it is difficult to achieve in formalized exchanges of information is "brain storming", (problem solving where a small team or only two people exchange ideas). These may often be verbalized as fragments of conversation which do not seem to make a lot of sense when transcribed and where leaps of logic are particularly fruitful. The term "on the same wave length" seems to imply the idea that the participants have evoked already existing, matching, world views. Hence, they need fewer words to refer to a concept that they share and may naturally relate concepts that they both consider are appropriate. Eventually they will arrive at a conclusion or solution that they both find satisfactory. This creative problem solving is not considered by this author to be tacit. It stems rather from having a compatible background and language of practice (a large degree of existing shared meaning) but is also stimulated by fast response and even interruption so that concepts are molded before "they set". Introna [1998] is concerned with the fact that cooperation needs this type of intimate and rich communication and that this will be impossible to achieve in technologically supported environments. This seems to point to Information4, which is tacit. Figure 3.1 illustrates the four types of information.

Making Information 3 explicit

When a person expresses Information3 as words, music or anything else, it becomes Information 2. It loses part of its context, its meaning is once again only potential, it may not be well expressed and hence be prone to misinterpretation. This is explained by Dahlbom and

Mathiassen [1995: 33] and illustrated in Figure 3.2, based on a diagram in De Villiers [1995: 83]. Mingers [1995], using Dreske's terminology, refers to this as making analogue information digital. Codified information, that is, Information1 is by definition already explicit and is, therefore, easy to copy and has little natural protection. Tacit information, because it is very difficult to capture and make explicit can be lost permanently when, for example, an experienced member of staff retires [Chesbrough & Teece, 1996].

3.2. SOURCES OF INFORMATION

Literature of a Subject is its Foundation. It represents a record of achievements of human race. Literature is diverse, Complex and multilingual in nature. It is becoming more and more inter-disciplinary. It is growing at a fast pace. In sciences, it is almost doubling itself in every very few years according to some studies. In social Sciences, it is doubling at the rate of every eight to twelve years. Literature serves the informational needs of various kinds of Users. It forms source of Information. Traditionally Specking, information Sources would include primarily books, periodicals and newspapers. However, the number and forms of source are continuously increasing. In addition, unpublished sources are becoming increasingly important to scholars. Occasions will arise, especially in a special library of University library, when information would be required by a user without precondition about the form of document. In such a situation, what matters is the finding of information not the sources of information.

What is Information Source : An Information Source is a source of information for somebody, i.e. anything that might informs a person about something on provide knowledge to somebody. Information sources may be observations, people speeches, documents, pictures, organizations etc.

Types of information sources : Different epistemologies have different views regarding the importance of different kind of information sources. Empiricism regards sense data as the ultimate information sources, while other epistemologies have different views (Kragh 1989). The various types of information sources can be divided into two broad categories.

A. DOCUMENTARY SOURCES

B. NON-DOCUMENTARY SOURCES

A. Documentary Sources

These are generally published or recorded documents of knowledge. Documentary sources may be as under :

Documentary sources of information

Primary	*Secondary*	*Tertiary*
Condensation & Repackaging	*Keys and aids to search*	
• Periodical	• Indexing Services	• Yearbooks & Directories
• Research Report	• Abstracting Services	• Bibliographies
• Conference Proceedings	• Review of Progress	• Location list of periodicals
• Patents	• Reference Works	
• Standards	• Treatises	• List of Indexing and abstracting services
• Trade Literature	• Monographs	
• Theses	• Text Books	• Guides
		• List of Research in progress
		• Guide to professional

A.1. Primary Sources

Primary sources of information are the first published records of original research and development or description of new application or new interpretation of an old theme or idea. There are original documents representing unfiltered original ideas.

These constitute the latest available information. A

researcher producing new information can make it available to the particular community through the primary sources. Often, it may be the only source of information in existence. Primary sources are unorganized sources, which are rather difficult to use by them, the secondary sources helps us to use these. These are important sources of information. A subject becomes a discipline in its own right when independent primary sources begin to be produced in that area. The rate of growth of a discipline to a large extent depends upon the amount of literature being produced in the form of primary sources reporting development in the concerned field.

Primary source is a term used in a number of disciplines to describe source material that is closest to the person, information, period or idea being studied.

In historiography, a primary source (also called original source) is an artifact, a document, a recording, or other source of information that was created at the time under study. If created by a human source then a source with direct personal knowledge of the events being described.

It serves as an original source of information about the topic. Similar definitions are used in library Science, and other areas of scholarship.

In journalism, a primary source can be a person with direct knowledge of a situation or a document created by such a person. Primary sources are distinguished from secondary sources, which cite, comment on, or build upon primary sources, though the distinction is not a sharp one. "Primary and secondary are relative terms, with sources judged primary or secondary according to specific historical contexts and what is being studied." (Kragh 1989)

For Example :

- Books
- Periodicals

- Conference Papers
- Research Monographs
- Research Reports
- Patents
- Standards
- Thesis
- Industrial and trade literature
- Manuscripts
- Unpublished Sources:- Memoranda Laboratory notebooks
    a. Diaries
    b. Company Files
    c. Portraits
    d. State Papers
- Web sites
- Video Recordings Speeches
- Works of Arts, architecture, literature and music.

A.2. Secondary Sources

Secondary sources of information are those which are either compiled from or refer to primary sources of information. The original information having been casually modified selected or reorganized so as to serve a definite purpose for group of users. Such sources contain information arranged and organized on the basis of some definite plan. These contain organized repackaged knowledge rather than new knowledge. Information given in primary sources is made available in a more convenient form. Due to their very nature, secondary sources are more easily and widely available than primary sources. These not only provide digested information but also serve as bibliographical key to primary sources of information. The primary sources are the first to appear, these are followed by secondary sources. It is difficult to find information from primary sources directly. Therefore, one should consult the secondary sources in the first instance, which will lead one to specific primary sources.

A.2.1. Kinds of secondary sources

"Bonn" has divided the secondary sources into three types which are as below

1. Index Type:
   a. Index
   b. Bibliography
   c. Indexing periodicals
   d. Abstracting Periodicals
2. Survey Type:
   a. Review
   b. Treatise
   c. Monograph
3. Reference Type:
   a. Encyclopedia
   b. Dictionary
   c. Hand book, Manual
   d. Critical Tables

Important ones are discussed below :

1. Periodicals : All periodicals do not report original work. There are a number of periodicals which specialize in interpreting and providing opinions on developments reported in primary sources of information. Such periodicals may be considered secondary sources.

e.g. *New Society* (1962). London: New Science Application. Weekly.

2. Indexes : An Index to a work contains an alphabetical list of names, topics, places, formulae, titles of any significant item referring to material presented in the main part of the work. Sometimes, these items may be arranged chronologically, geographically or in some other way. A well compiled index adds to usefulness of a work.

e.g. *Index of Economic Journals*(1961-62).Homewood III. Irwin: American Economic Association. 5 Vols.

3. Bibliographies : A bibliography is an organized list of primary or other sources relating to a given subject or person. It is usually arranged alphabetically by author or chronologically or topic wise. It may be comprehensive or selective. Sometimes it may be provided with annotations. It may be published as a part of a larger work or as a separate work. The basic aim of a bibliography is to assist the users in locating the existence of or identifying a book or any other material which may be interest to him. A well prepared bibliography provides a definite coverage of documents over a period of time within specified limits. Thus, it also serves the purpose of retrospective searching of literature,

e.g. Griffith, Dudley David (1955), *Bibliography of Chaucer, 1908-53.* Seattle: University of Washington Press.

4. Indexing Periodicals : An Indexing Periodical is a regularly issued compilation of titles of articles that appear in current primary source journals. Generally, titles of new books pamphlets etc. are also included. An index to a publication contains an alphabetical list of names, topics, places, formulate, titles of any significant items referring to material presented in the main part of the work. These items are arranged chronologically, geographically or in some other way. An indexing periodical is a regularly issued compilation of titles of articles that appear in current primary source journals, generally titles of new books, pamphlets are also included.

e.g., *Reader's guide to periodical literature* (1905). New York: Wilson. vol-1. Semi -monthly.

5. Abstracting Periodicals : Abstracts appear in different formats. The best known format for abstracting services is periodical. An abstracting periodical "is a regularly issued compilation of concise summaries of (i) significant articles (often in a very limited subject field) that appear in current primary sources journals and (ii) important new research monographs, reports, patents and other primary source publication in that field." (Bonne, George S.1971)

An Abstracting Periodical serves as an index, a tool for retrieval of information on a specific subject. However indexing periodicals are earlier to appear than abstracting periodicals.

6. Reviews (Survey Type) : A review is a survey of the primary literature. It aims to digest and correlate the literature over a given period. It also indicates the development and trends in the field concerned. It may appear as a collection of papers on regular basis (annual or quarterly or monthly) or in the form of an article in a periodical. A review provides background information to a new problem in a suitable form and serves as a key to literature. List of references given in a review can serve as first rate bibliography of the concerned subject for a period covered by it,

e.g. *Annual review of biochemistry* (1932) Palo Alto: Annual Reviews. Annual.

7. Reference Books (also considered tertiary) : Reference works, which contain the desired information itself, are considered secondary sources of information. These include encyclopedias, dictionaries, handbooks, tables, formularies etc. these form an important part of secondary sources of information. The sources of ready reference books are as follows-:

(a) ***Dictionaries* :** A dictionary is a book, which deals with words of a language or of some special subjects, authors, etc. Thus a dictionary is a wordbook. Although a dictionary is supposed to deal with words but often it may go beyond this.

e.g. *Webster's third new International dictionary of English language unabridged with seven language dictionary* (1966). Spring field: Mass, Merriam.

(b) ***Encyclopedias (also considered tertiary)*** **:** An encyclopedia is a book giving information on all branches of knowledge or a specific subject. It is an ideal book, which deals with concepts. An encyclopedia is a storehouse of knowledge giving all information of significance. However, it is best used for finding answers to background questions related to general information and self-education. One often turns to encyclopedias for one's everyday information requirements. This is also true of scientists and technologists.

e.g. *Encyclopaedia Americana (1976).* New York: Grolier. 30 vols.

(c) ***Handbook*** **:** A handbook is a compilation of miscellaneous information in a compact and handy form. It contains data, procedures, principles, including tables, graphs, diagrams and illustrations. Scientists and technologists use handbooks in their fields rather frequently.

e.g. *Britain, (1948/49) an official handbook.* London: stationary office, annual.

(d) ***Tables*** **:** Many of the handbooks contain data in the form of tables. Some of the handbooks devote substantial portion of the work to tables as compared with text. Tables are convent form to present data. There are extremely useful in Science.

e.g. *Tables of contents and numerical data* (1947). Oxford: Pergamon Press.Vol.1

(e) ***Manuals*** **:** In common practice, a manual is an instruction book, which instructs how to do something by means of specific and clear directions.

e.g. Greenly, R.S.(1974). *Professional Investor's Manual.* London: Greenly.

(f) ***Magazine and newspaper articles (this distinction varies by discipline)*** : A news article is an article Published in a print of Internet news medium such as a newspaper, newsletter news magazine, news oriented website, or article directory that discusses current or recent news of either general interest (i.e. daily newspapers) or on a specific topic (i.e. political or trade news magazines, club newsletters, or technology news websites).

8. Text Books (other than fiction and autobiography) : A textbook is a book of instruction. Its Primary aim is not to impart information about a specific subject but to enable one to develop proper understanding of the subject. Presentation is extremely important and it is prepared to serve a particular level of readership. It cannot be comprehensive. Often presentation is colorful and attractive, giving plenty of illustrations and diagrams. A good textbook takes into consideration the method of teaching and level of readership. It is revised keeping in view new developments and changing methodology of teaching. There is a difference of opinion about the place of text books as tertiary sources.

e.g. Text Book of Crop Production, by P.C. Rahaja, etc Bombay,

9. Translations : Translations are an important part of secondary sources. Their characteristics are the same as those of primary or secondary or tertiary sources from which these are translated. Many of the authors of research papers prefer to cite original sources rather than translations.

10. Treatises : A Treatise is a comprehensive compilation or summary of information on a subject. A treatise on a subject provides enough information to a person to acquire basic knowledge, so essential for carrying out advanced research. It also provides facts, along with discussion. The fact may include physical constants methods of preparation and purification of compounds etc. Usually, it is limited to a broad field. Due to the very nature, these become out of date within a short period of time.

e.g. *Treatise on the calculus of finite differences*(1960). 4th ed. New York: Chelsa.

11. Monographs : A monograph is a short treatise on a specific subject. A monograph and treaties serve the same purposes with the difference that a monograph is an attempt on a limited scale. Very often a monograph may be brought out as a part of series. e.g Baldwin,E. (1971). *Study In The History Of Ideas* (Monographer in arts and archeology series, 25). Princeton, N.J: Princeton university press.

12. Biographical words : A biography is a description or account of someone's life and the times, which is usually published in the form of a book or an essay, or in some other form, such as a film. An autobiography (auto meaning "self", giving "self-biography") is a biography of a person's life written or told by that same person. A biography is more than a list of impersonal facts (education, work, relationship and death), it also portrays the subject's experience of those events. Unlike a profile or curriculum vitae (resume), a biography presents the subject's story, highlighting various aspects of his or her life, including intimate details of experiences, and may include as analysis of the subject's personality.

13. Literary criticism : It is the study, evaluation and interpretation of literature. Modern Literary criticism is often informed by literary theory, which is the philosophical discussion of its methods and goals. Though the two activities are closely related, literary critics are not always, and have not always been, theorists.

A.3. Tertiary Sources

This is the most problematic category of all. However, people rarely expected to differentiate between secondary and tertiary sources. Materials in which the information from secondary sources has been digested- reformatted and condensed, to put it into a convenient, easy to read form. Sources which are once removed in time from secondary sources and works which index, organize and compile citations to, and show you how to use, secondary sources.

Tertiary sources of information contain information distilled and collected from primary and secondary sources. The primary function of tertiary sources of information is to aid the searcher of information in the use of primary and secondary sources of information. Most of these sources do not contain subject knowledge. Due to increase in literature, tertiary sources are becoming increasingly important. Out of various kinds of sources, tertiary sources are the last to appear.

Types

1. Bibliography of Bibliographies
2. Directories and yearbooks
3. Guide to literature
4. List of research in progress

B. Non-documentary Sources

Non documentary sources of information form a substantial part of communication especially in science and technology. User's studies have underlined importance of such sources. These sources provide information which other sources do not.

Types : There are two kinds of sources:-

1. Formal Sources

- Research Organization
- Societies
- Industries
- Govt. departments.

- Universities
- Consultants

2. Informal Sources

- Conversation with colleges
- Visitors
- Attendance at Professional Meetings.

The above categorization is based on the characteristics of the documents. Primary sources are more current and accurate than secondary and tertiary. In searching for Information, a researcher usually starts with secondary and tertiary sources and ends the search with primary sources. Secondary and tertiary sources contain information in organized form and these serve as guides or indicators to detailed contents of primary literature. With increasing amount of literature being produced, it is becoming almost impossible to use primary sources directly for searching of information. A scholar would also not be able to keep himself up to date and well informed in his field of specialization without the aid of secondary and tertiary sources. This goes to show the importance of these sources of information.

3.3. REFERENCE AND INFORMATION SERVICES

In this first decade of the twenty-first century reference and information services are a vital yet changing part of the function and mission of the library institution. While the continually expanding availability of electronic resources and digitized materials has changed the nature of reference, the essential service remains central. Indeed, far from minimizing the need for reference services, the rise of the Internet, and with it the availability of a tremendous number of subscription and free online resources, makes this aspect of library service all the more crucial. Librarians and their users are constantly bombarded with a wide range of information choices that must be evaluated for authenticity and accuracy. Whether at home on their computers or wandering through the stacks, many people feel as though they are drowning in a sea of information. New media and technologies are like tributaries leading to this great new body of knowledge, and each stream makes the waters deeper and more perilous. Reference services are at once a life raft, map, and compass to those who feel adrift. In providing them with a combination of personalized service in a timely manner, libraries reaffirm their centrality as twenty-first century public institutions par excellence.

For all its contemporary relevance, the concept of reference service is more than a century old. In 1876, Samuel Green, librarian of the Worcester Free Public Library in Massachusetts, developed the idea of having librarians assist the user in the selection of books to suit their needs. This served a dual function, increasing the use of his library's collection and thereby demonstrating the need for the library. Green saw the role of the public library as one of welcoming users by having a pleasant and cultivated female staff (Genz, 1998). Some forty years later, in 1915 at the thirty-seventh meeting of the American Library Association, a paper on reference work was delivered by W.W. Bishop, the superintendent of the Reading Room of the Library of Congress. Bishop defined reference work as "the service rendered by a librarian in aid of some sort of study" holding that it was "an organized effort on the part of libraries in aid of the most expeditious and fruitful use of their books." (Genz, 1998: 511)

The idea of reference service was further developed by Charles Williamson in his 1923 report, "Training for Library Service: A Report Prepared for the Carnegie Corporation of New York," which included a course description for reference work:

A study of the standard works of reference, general and special encyclopedias, dictionaries, annuals, indexes to periodicals, ready reference manuals of every kind, special bibliographies, and the more important newspapers and periodicals. Works of similar scope are compared, and the limitations of each pointed out. Lists of questions made up from practical experience are given, and the method of finding the answers discussed in the class. (Genz, 1998: 513)

Several authors, including James I. Wyer, Margaret Hutchins, William A. Katz, Richard E. Bopp, and Linda C. Smith wrote reference texts in which they continued to refine the role of the reference librarian over the subsequent decades. Perhaps the most important point to remember is that reference service seeks to fulfill the greater mission of the library by helping individual users. Despite the many transformations that have been wrought on reference work by both developments of our information society and paradigm shifts in the self understandings of the library, much has remained the same. First and foremost, it is still a service in which the librarian interacts with a patron on a one-to-one basis. This level of personal service has become even more important in the twenty-first century in light of the alienating and depersonalizing effects of many information technologies. On the other hand, the way such service is provided has changed considerably—it now extends beyond face-to-face assistance thanks to the availability of the telephone, e-mail, and the technology for chat and IM reference.

3.3.1. Ethical Awareness and Engagement

Ethical awareness and engagement is a crucial aspect of all library services, and the ideals that have been established for the profession generally apply fully to those working in reference services. Just as therapists would do their patients little good if they did not keep their information confidential, reference librarians must follow certain standards of behavior if the service they provide is to be effective. The American Library Association's current Code of Ethics, adopted in 1995, provides a useful guide. This code, composed of eight broad statements, upholds a variety of the principles essential to the modern library.

The first statement of the Code insists that librarians should provide the "highest level of service to all library users" and service that is equitable for all with information provided that is "accurate, unbiased and courteous." This statement is at the heart of good reference service, which strives to provide good quality information and information that can be documented. Reference staff must understand what constitutes a good reference interaction and must strive to meet that standard with each user query (Bunge, 1999).

The second statement of the Code calls for the protection of the "principles of intellectual freedom" and resistance to "all efforts to censor library resources." Library selection is reflected in this statement, as librarians attempt to provide information on a subject from many points of view. The third statement protects the user's right to privacy and confidentiality in requesting and using library resources. Reference librarians must be particularly cognizant of this professional obligation. They must respect the privacy of a user by keeping their reference interview and the resources used confidential.

According to the fourth statement, intellectual property rights should be recognized and respected. It is important that librarians keep current with changes in intellectual property laws, especially copyright, and keep their users aware of these laws. Librarians must know when copying is covered under the "fair use" provision of the law and when copying violates the copyright law. This is more than a good in itself; it also helps protect the institution, its employees, and its users from claims of copyright infringement and intellectual dishonesty. The fifth through the eighth statements of the Code all treat the relationship between personal interests and professional responsibilities.

The fifth encourages the respectful treatment of coworkers and colleagues and the safeguarding of the rights of all employees. This is a statement that encompasses the whole library and its staff. Every staff member should ensure that others are treated fairly.

In the sixth statement, library employees are cautioned not to put private interests ahead of library interests. This means that employees should be circumspect in their dealings with library vendors and others outside the library so their decisions are made on professional merit and are not influenced by personal interest.

The seventh statement cautions library employees not to put personal convictions or beliefs ahead of library interests. This is also of special significance to reference librarians. Sometimes a librarian must help a user research an area that is personally against the librarian's beliefs or philosophy. But by putting professional duties first, the librarian can successfully assist the user and provide the information needed.

The eighth statement encourages all library staff to continue to grow in their knowledge and skills and to assist those entering the profession. We live in a time when change is constant, so all library staff must continue to learn and change.

Other professional library organizations have their own codes of ethics. These include the American Society for Information Science (ASIS), the Society of American Archivists, the Medical Library Association, and the American Association of Law Libraries.

3.3.2. Kinds of Information Service

Information service, in the most general sense, is the process of assisting library users to identify sources of information in response to a particular question, interest, assignment, or problem. Sometimes referred to as reference service, the Reference and User Services

Association (RUSA) of the American Library Association defines reference transactions as "information consultations in which library staff recommend, interpret, evaluate, and/or use information resources to help others to meet particular information needs" (*www.ala.org/ala/mgrps/divs/rusa/resources/guidelines/definitions reference.cfm*). These reference transactions can take place in person or via the telephone, e-mail, or virtual reference technologies. Librarians are also creating Web sites, answer archives, and links to answers to "frequently asked questions" all designed to anticipate user questions and help people find information independently. Traditional reference desk service continues to be highly valued by library users in many settings, but the newer forms continue to grow in popularity. Consequently, it is all the more important that librarians understand the range of inquiries that can be expected, allowing them to provide a full and ready answer, regardless of the form in which the query arises.

3.3.3. Current Awareness Service (CAS)

Dissemination of information that will keep it users well-informed and up-to-date in their fields of basic interest as well as in related subjects is called Current Awareness Service. It is a system of getting knowledge on recent development, and especially those developments which relate to the special interest of the individual.

CAS is a device of the information system through which the users of information can be informed promptly, as soon as possible after publications but before absorption into the comprehensive secondary sources of current literature on a broad subject field or on an area in which a group of persons are interested, and presented in a manner, volume and rhythm intended to facilitate or cultivate current approach to information.

CAS involves knowledge of

i. New theoretical ideas and hypotheses.

ii. New problems to be solved.

iii. New methods and techniques for solving old and new problems

iv. New circumstances affecting what people do and how they may do it.

Dr. S.R. Ranganathan defines CAS as "Documentation periodical listing the documents appearing during the period covered, and without being selected to suit the requirements of a particular reader or of a specific topic under investigation. It endeavours to keep the clientele informed promptly of all the nascent thought created in their fields of work and related fields."

B.C. Vickery defines "CAS is more frequently and more adequately met by circulation than by retrieval, current journals, newly received book and report, abstract bulletins and the like being fed to and scanned by users."

Basically, speaking, CAS is a device for alerting specialists towards latest developments and new publications acquired by the libraries/information centre. So, we can define CAS as- "The establishment of a system for reviewing/scanning, publications immediately upon receipt, selecting information pertinent to the needs of the organization served, and recording/notifying individual items of interest to be brought to the attention of those persons to whose work they are related."

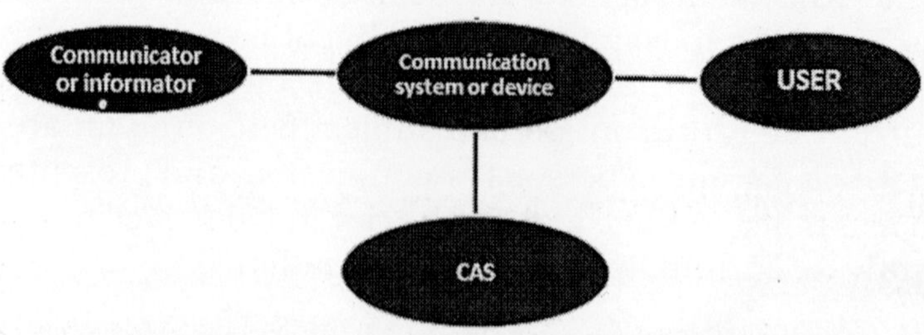

In view of the above, CAS is a direct link between the user and the communicator through communication system or communication devices. This system or device is called Current Awareness Service.

Types of Current Awareness Service

Two kinds of Current Awareness Services may be recognised.

I. Those services, which are directed towards individuals or group of users. These may include communication of information to individuals or groups through informal conversation or via telephone, a message sent on notification form, SDI, selective of dissemination of documents, routeing of periodicals (or automatic loan) and other documents. In this field, information supplied within the period of one week to one month.

II. Those services, which are directed towards all users of the services, these may include accession list (a list of recent acquisitions), bibliography, indexing and abstracting services, bibliographic surveys, literature surveys, table of contents of periodicals received in the library, Current Awareness bulletin, etc. in this field, information supplied daily or within the period of one week.

Aims and Purposes of Current Awareness Service

i. To aware the scientists/users with latest developments in their subject fields.

ii. To keep the clientele well-informed and up-to-date knowledge of latest development in their fields of research.

iii. To fulfil the current demand of the users.

3.3.4. Selective Dissemination Of Information (SDI)

Originally a phrase related to library and information Science, SDI refers to tools and resources used to keep a user informed of new resources on specified topics. SDI services pre-date the World Wide Web, and the term itself is somewhat dated. Contemporary analogous systems for SDI services include alerts, current awareness tools or trackers. These systems provide automated searches that inform the user of the availability of new resources meeting the user's specified keywords and search parameters. Alerts can be received a number of ways, including email, RSS feeds, voice mail, Instant messaging, and text messaging. Selective dissemination of information was a concept first described by Hans Peter Luhn of IBM in the 1950s. Software was developed in many companies and in government to provide this service in the 1950s and 60s, which allowed distribution of items recently published in abstract journals to be routed to individuals who are likely to be interested in the contents. For example, the system at Ft. Monmouth automatically sent out (by mail) a different set of abstracts to each of about 1,000 scientists and engineers in the army depending on what they were working on. The selection was based on an "interest profile," a list of keywords that described their interests. In some organizations, the 'interest profile' was much more than a simple list of keywords. Librarians or information professionals conducted extensive interviews with their clients to establish a fairly complex profile for each individual. Based on these profiles, the information professionals would then distribute selectively appropriate information to their clients A selective dissemination of information (SDI) system attempts to facilitate users' information retrieval and information filtering needs. With the rise of the internet as an information source, the volume of information available ranging across all interests has exploded, and difficulties in surveying, querying, and filtering information pertaining to individuals' interests increase with this explosion. The goal of an SDI system is to deliver new information arriving at an SDI-aware information provider to users who express their interests via user profiles. Mechanisms used to implement such SDI systems vary; one such option is a persistent query mechanism. Users create and pose queries to an SDI system; queries remain resident in the system which works to somehow match documents and users. Successful matches are delivered from the SDI system back to users.

Process of SDI

Selective Dissemination of Information (SDI) Service is a refinement of CAS service which is directed to individual / personal requirement (personalized). It provides a deeper analysis of literature. If two people exactly match in terms of their interest, then SDI also can be provided to the two people.

Steps in SDI : The steps in providing SDI services are same as that of CAS, the difference is only in the depth of the interest. So, the steps involved in SDI may be of the following types

(a) ***Creation of User Profile*** **:** The profiles of the user, who are to be given CAS service, are prepared. A profile may consist of the following fields and can be noted down in a database or Microsoft Excel sheet.

i. Name

ii. Designation

iii. Subject

iv. Keywords that collectively characterize the subject interest of an individual.

v. Email Id

vi. Mobile Number

vii. Fax

viii. Complete postal address, etc

The first four fields will identify the person and the last four fields will be used to deliver the CAS to the user. The profile can be of a single user or a group working on the same project or some limited subject field. The profile obtained thus must be kept up-to-date. Therefore, if the topic of inertest changes then the corresponding profile must also be modified accordingly. In some organizations, the interest profile was much more than a simple list of keywords. Librarians or information professionals conducted extensive interviews with their clients to establish a fairly complex profile for each individual.

(b) ***Acquisition of Resources*** **:** The different sources of information, periodicals, research papers, which are relevant to the parent body, must be selected and collected from different sources. In the next step, through rapid reading the resources are scanned by the LIS professionals to find out the key concepts.

(c) ***Creation of Document Profile*** **:** The relevant and significant information is recorded in the form of content list for different contexts. The recorded information may be in the form of an abstract or an extract. Depending upon the significance of the document, the bibliographical details and indexing terms and the information itself are stored on the file / magnetic tape / computer document.

(d) ***Matching Profile*** **:** In a regular interval, the user profile should be correlated or matched with the document profile. The computer compares the two inputs; the output is printed out in the form of two cards. One card is called information card that contain either the list of document or the information itself along with bibliographical details of document which also has a tear off strip request note. The other card is called response card.

(e) ***Notification / Information Communication*** **:** If there exists any matching between the two profiles then the matching information is sent to the user or

group of users, who may require it, through different means of communication in anticipation, like telephone calls, postal mail / email / SMS with a request to call at the reference desk to get the pertinent information. In case of postal communication, the two cards are sent to the user. The information can also be sent through a messenger.

(f) ***Feedback Mechanism*** **:** The user keeps the information card for his use. In case he wants to consult the document, he tears off the request note strip and sends it to the library along with the response card, in which he indicates the degree of interest in the particular document.

(g) ***Library Action*** **:** The library takes action on the request note strip to send the document(s) to the concerned user or to keep it in the library for him. The response card helps the library to know about the usefulness of the information provided as well as the shift in the information need. The library accordingly modifies the user profile page for improving performance.

3.3.4. Answering Reference Questions

In light of the immense diversity and range of possible questions, being approached by a patron with a reference need can seem like a daunting prospect. Indeed, much of the difficulty of information services arises from uncertainty about the kind of service or breadth of information called for by a given question. Categorizing reference questions by type is a useful way to make sense of such concerns. Three common types of information service are ready reference questions, research questions, and bibliographic verification.

Ready reference questions such as “Where was Abraham Lincoln born?” “Who won the 1992 World Series?” “What is the capital of Nicaragua?” or “Where can I find a copy of the United States' Declaration of Independence?" can be readily answered using one or two general reference sources. The librarian may be tempted to tell the user the answer to simple ready reference questions. Yet here the old saying that "giving a man a fish feeds him for a day while teaching him to fish feeds him for a lifetime" is proven true. No matter how simple they seem initially, ready reference questions provide the possibility of teachable moments. Whenever possible, librarians should lead users through the process of looking up the information rather than simply providing the solution.

Librarians who assist users with ready reference inquiries on a regular basis sometimes choose to create a "ready reference" section of the most commonly used resources either in print or on the library's Web site to answer quick questions. Typically, such sections include a general all-purpose encyclopaedias, dictionaries, almanacs, and handbooks. Care must be taken to keep the sources up-to-date and to avoid depending so heavily on this subset of the collection that other sources are overlooked by library users and librarians. Librarians may find that ready reference questions have diminished due to the ease of answering basic questions through online information portals such as Google. Nevertheless, ready reference remains a cornerstone of information services, and librarians should be primed to provide it at any time.

Research questions are more complex, may take much longer to answer, and typically require multiple sources of information. These questions often require the user to consider a variety of sources and viewpoints and to subsequently draw conclusions. Sometimes questions that initially seem like ready reference questions are far more complex as previously hidden facets of the user's inquiry are revealed. Here, the variety of possible sources increases with the complexity of users' questions. Librarians should, for example, guide the user in the use of bibliographic sources, citations, and the back-of-the-book bibliographies. Likewise, users with complex questions may need to be taught how to find or request the full text of articles for which only citations are given in a search of electronic databases, allowing them to move beyond cursory surveys of the literature.

Research questions, especially if the user is unable to fully articulate the nature of his or her query, require librarians to ask questions of their own, trying to get at the nature of the request before setting out to help the patron answer it. The librarian may, for example, have to determine how much information is needed, what level of information is needed, and what other sources have already been consulted. As will be discussed in Chapter 3, information services call for mutual engagement, especially with more complex questions. Reference librarians should never be passive participants, pointing the way to an answer. Instead, they should play the part of dynamic guides, joining users on their journeys to knowledge.

Naturally, the extent of such engagement may vary from one circumstance to another. Different types of libraries tend to have their own standards for how long librarians should spend with users on research questions. Many public libraries recommend that users be given five or ten minutes of personal assistance and then asked to return if more help is needed. A university library may have a similar standard, or depending on the institution, may be able to invite the user to make an appointment for more in-depth research assistance. Some libraries may suggest that users call or e-mail ahead of their visit so the librarian can be prepared to offer the best possible assistance. Other libraries, including special libraries, may only be able to provide a basic level of help during the first visit. Libraries may refer users to other libraries with more specialized materials in the area of the user's research or may offer to call back if additional information is found.

Finally a library user may seek bibliographic verification when he or she has already obtained the information needed but must verify the sources. Sometimes this service is a matter of fact checking, whereas on other occasions users may have completed their research but lack full citation information. As users increasingly depend on electronic databases for information, compiling and formatting bibliographic citations becomes easier. Verifying and citing material found on Web pages is more difficult since the information needed for the citation is not always easy to find.

3.3.5. Reader's Advisory Service

Reader's advisory service, sometimes considered a type of information service, is the quest to put the right book in the hands of the right reader. Librarians are increasingly expected to provide an answer to the dreaded question, "Can you help me find a good book?" Fortunately, as demand has increased, so too has the ease of providing this service. Although there is no substitute for one's own knowledge or experience, many new technologies serve to make the reader's advisory far easier than it was in the past. Many online databases, for example, have functions that automatically recommend other books for those who like a given title. Others have searchable lists of works by genre, helping readers match their favourite books to others like them. As always, however, remember that reader's advisory, like other reference work, is predicated on the interaction between librarian and library user. Asking directed questions, listening carefully to the users' responses, and tailoring assistance accordingly is the basis of excellent, truly helpful service.

The reader's advisory service is generally associated with public libraries and tends to be employed primarily by those looking for fiction. In academic libraries, it is far less common as users rarely come in searching for a mystery to read. Even so, reader's advisory may be needed to help lay researchers looking to deepen their knowledge of a particular field. A patron who has read and enjoyed Stephen Ambrose's Undaunted Courage, but is troubled by allegations about Ambrose's questionable accuracy and academic honesty, may want to know the titles of books about the Lewis and Clark expedition that are both reputable and engaging. Successful reader's advisory librarians are skilled at asking users questions that enable them to assess users' reading level, language, or educational background. They must know a great deal about various genres of fiction and nonfiction and be intimately familiar with their library's collection. Significantly, it is important that they be able to convey their expertise in a friendly and conversational manner. Truly mastering reader's advisory service requires a great deal of skill and practice.

3.3.6. Information Literacy

User instruction, which is now usually referred to as information literacy, may range from showing an individual how to use the library's online catalog and basic print reference sources to formal classroom sessions about conducting research in the library. The basic component of information literacy includes demonstrating how, when, and why to use various reference sources in an integrated way that will capture the user's attention at the teachable moment.

In today's educational settings, the ease of using electronic resources often results in a failure to teach more traditional research strategies. While finding superficial information has grown easier, in-depth information has become increasingly obscure for many students. In the library too, approaches to instruction may vary and librarians often question whether to simply answer questions posed by users or to teach users how to employ the available resources. This may be contingent on the mission or purpose of the library. Academic institutions may call on their librarians to help students understand how to engage effectively and independently in the research and information evaluation process. Public librarians, by contrast, may try to teach users about reference sources in a more informal manner as they lead users to the answers they seek. Thus, while instruction is always an important part of reference work, the degree to which they go about providing it is highly contingent on the circumstances.

In any case, all reference librarians must be skilled at helping users find information and answers quickly and be ready to teach users how to use the reference sources that are available. The best reference librarians develop an intuition for when to be information providers and when to be bibliographic instructors. In some libraries, only specific, designated librarians are charged with conducting library instruction courses. Nevertheless, an increasing number of librarians are required to participate in their libraries' bibliographic instruction program, and library school graduates are expected to be capable of teaching basic classes on the use of library resources. As should be clear, even those librarians not charged with providing formal instruction have the opportunity to teach those they serve.

3.3.7. Selecting and Evaluating Print and Electronic Information

Selecting and evaluating print and electronic information for the library's collection can be as professionally rewarding as providing expert information service. Reference librarians' involvement in evaluating and selecting titles for the collection helps them develop rich knowledge of the sources at their disposal, increasing their effectiveness.

The responsibility for selecting reference materials depends largely on the size and scope of the library. In large academic libraries, selecting reference materials may be assigned to subject bibliographers whose work may be limited to collection development responsibilities. On the other side of the continuum, the evaluation and purchase of resources in very small libraries may be the work of a single reference librarian or coordinator of reference. A range of shared evaluation and selection possibilities between these points include reference materials selection committees or group assignments.

The question, "What makes a book a reference book?" has long been debated in our profession. For the purpose of this discussion, reference books are those texts set aside to be consulted for specific information rather than to be read as a whole. In other words, reference books contain content meant to be "looked up." Typically, one turns to a reference source in search of something in particular rather than to the text as a whole. Another common characteristic of reference books is that they do not leave the library premises. This ensures that all works in the reference collection are always on hand, making for a consistently available body of knowledge. Note that labeling narrative or non-reference books as "reference" to deter theft or ensure that a popular volume is always available may lead to bloated reference collections, and it is not generally recommended. Finally, with the addition of electronic reference sources, which are increasingly available to remote library users from their homes, dorm rooms, offices, and elsewhere, reference collections encompass much more than print books and serials and may be available twenty-four hours a day.

As the present trend toward shrinking budgets for reference collections, lean reference collections, and the elimination of duplication among print and electronic collections continues, the careful evaluation and selection of reference materials is essential. Libraries should determine the criteria that will be used in selecting sources for its reference collection. The following criteria may help determine whether an item is a worthy addition to a library's collection: scope, quality of content, appropriateness for audience, format, arrangement, authority, currency, and accuracy, ease of use, unique coverage and cost. Criteria for selecting electronic resources may vary, though all of the criteria used to evaluate print resources should be considered, especially in libraries that aim to avoid redundancy in their print and electronic reference collections.

Some libraries select reference materials by reading reviews in the library professional literature such as Library Journal and Choice and Booklist's "Reference Books Bulletin." Other institutions insist on physically reviewing reference sources at trade shows or through special arrangements with publishers of reference materials. Most libraries employ a combination of these two.

3.3.8. Creating Finding Tools and Web Sites

Another strategy employed by many reference departments is the creation of finding tools and pathfinders for library users. Here, librarians act as cartographers, mapping out the best routes through familiar territory and pointing out interesting sites along the way. Pathfinders are often prepared for commonly requested subjects such as high school and college assignments about capital punishment, drug abuse, and the history of Native American tribes. Similarly, public libraries may prepare pathfinders that address frequently asked questions of a quotidian nature such as: finding job information, checking the credentials of a health care provider, or researching a family tree. Depending on the topic, audience, and needs, the pathfinder may guide the user to a selection of appropriate reference books, relevant databases and search terms, a selection of current and authoritative Web sites, and tips for searching the library's Online Public Access Catalogue (OPAC) for additional materials.

Librarians also create Web sites of carefully evaluated links organized by topic, sometimes known as "webliographies" that serve as finding tools. Who better than librarians to organize the World Wide Web of information, pointing the users to "the best" sources and helping them steer clear of the dubious? Web-based finding tools offer several advantages to print pathfinders. They are available to users 24/7, they can be updated as often as needed, and they can include direct links to Web sites and electronic reference tools.

Depending on the circumstance and the nature of a library's Web presence such webliographies can be either general, providing direction to broadly targeted reference resources, or subject specific. General all-purpose lists of librarian-selected Web resources include the Internet Public Library (www.ipl.org) and the Librarians' Internet Index (lii.org). Examples of library subject-specific webliographies include The New York Public Library's Best of the Web (www .nypl.org/links/) and the University of Washington's Information Gateway (www.lib.washington.edu/subject/). Larger libraries, whether academic or public, often produce indexes of both types. Smaller libraries may be better served by developing webliographies for specific areas in which they have subject specialists and linking to a general reference site like the Internet Public Library or the Librarians' Internet Index.

3.3.9. Promoting and Marketing Libraries and Reference Service

Paying attention to promotion and marketing of libraries and reference service is becoming more important than ever. Without support from the community, the library will not stay viable. Promoting reference services among individual library users can go a long way toward achieving this goal, especially insofar as it demonstrates how the library can serve them. In large communities—urban public libraries, for example—promoting the library through individual users is not enough to attract new users and major marketing or publicity campaigns become important. In academic libraries, school libraries, and special libraries, promotion and marketing are equally essential. Use of print and online newsletters, Web sites, and opportunities to meet with faculty and staff can provide opportunities to promote the library's resources.

3.3.10. Evaluating Staff and Services

Libraries may seek to routinely evaluate their reference collections or reference service. In her book Evaluating Reference Services: A Practical Guide (Whitlatch, 2000: 1), Jo Bell Whitlatch wisely emphasizes the importance of defining the purpose of the evaluation before setting a strategy. "The most important questions you must ask," according to Whitlatch, are these: "Why am I evaluating reference services" and "What do I plan to do with the study results?"

The quality of the reference interaction, from either the user's or the librarian's perspective, may be assessed to help determine how effective the reference service is. Evaluating reference staff is one way to help determine how effective the reference service is, and is one way to help assure quality reference service. The American Library Association's Reference and User Services Association has developed "Guidelines for Behavioural Performance of Reference and Information Service Professionals," which are intended to be used in the training, development, or evaluation of library professionals and staff. The performance of reference librarians is typically evaluated on both the information conveyed to users and the satisfaction of the interaction on the library user. The following factors are covered by the ALA Guidelines:

Approachability : Are users able to identify that a reference librarian is available to help?

Interest : Does the librarian demonstrate a high degree of interest in the reference transaction?

Listening/Inquiring : Does the librarian identify the user's information need in a manner that puts the user at ease? Are good communication skills used throughout the transaction?

Searching : Is the librarian skilled at creating search strategies that yield accurate and relevant results?

Follow-up : Does the librarian determine if the user is satisfied with the results of the search/interaction?

These performance guidelines may form the backbone of a library's staff evaluation instruments, whether the instrument is a simple self-evaluation checklist, a peer-evaluation tool, or a formal evaluation system influencing earning potential. In addition to evaluating staff, the library may measure its productivity or efficiency with quantitative measures that include the number of questions answered and the frequency with which print and/or electronic sources are consulted. Smaller libraries may continuously count the number and type of in-person questions answered by the reference staff. In larger libraries, quarterly one-week periods are frequently used to estimate the number of questions answered over the course of a year. Depending on the available resources, data may be recorded using hand-held computers, by making hash marks on a form, or by any means in between.

A variety of other evaluation strategies are also available to libraries: Assessing the quality of the resources available may, for example, be another useful measurement. Issues of resource allocation may also be incorporated into departmental evaluations, if one includes how the library's budget allocates for library staff, print and electronic resources, computers and networks, and buildings. Evaluation methods frequently used to gauge users' satisfaction with reference services and sources include questionnaires, surveys, focus groups, observation and interviews.

It is crucial that library administrators determine what is to be measured and against what standards before choosing the preferred method of evaluation. Many sources are available for detailed information on designing evaluation instruments for libraries. Selecting the best method, developing and field testing the instrument, administering the survey, questionnaire, or interview, planning the observation, avoiding interviewer bias and scores of ethical issues should be carefully considered. Analyzing data and developing conclusions and recommendations may require advanced training and in some cases evaluation experts are hired.

REFERENCES

1. Bonn, George S. (1971). Literature of Science and Technology. *Mc Graw Hill Encyclopedia of Science and Technology*,7, 614.
2. Bopp, Richard E., and Linda C. Smith. 2001. Reference and Information Services: An Introduction. Englewood, CO: Libraries Unlimited.
3. Checkland, P., and Holwell, S. (1997). *Information, Systems and Information Systems*, John Wiley, Chichester.
4. Dhiman, Anil K. &Yashoda Rani (2005). *Learn Information and Reference Sources and Services*. New Delhi: Ess Publication.
5. Genz, Marcella D. 1998. "Working the Reference Desk." Library Trends 46, no. 3 (Winter): 505–525.
6. Gorman, Michael. 2003. The Enduring Library: Technology, Tradition, and the Quest for Balance. Chicago: American Library Association
7. Hutchins, Margaret (1974*). Introduction to reference work* (p.10-15). Chicago: American Library Association.
8. Katz, William A. 2001. Introduction to Reference Work. 2 vols. New York: McGraw-Hill.

9. Kragh , Helge (1989) . *An Introduction To The Historiography Of Science.* Cambridge University Press.

10. Krishan Kumar. *Reference Service* .5th rev ed.(p.115-127). New Delhi : Vikas Publishing House.

11. Nolan, Christopher W. 1999. Managing the Reference Collection. Chicago: American Library Association.

12. Tyckoson, David A. 2001. "What Is the Best Model of Reference Service?" Library Trends 50, no. 2 (Fall): 183–196.

13. Whitlatch, Jo Bell. 2000. Evaluating Reference Services: A Practical Guide. Chicago: American Library Association.

4

Impact of ICT on Library & Information Science Education and Training

4.1. INTRODUCTION

Since the dawn of civilization man has been striving to explore the affinity. On the long voyage of exploration man has collected innumerable objects as per requirement and tried to preserve them, undoubtedly a very fundamental attitude of mankind that initiated the concept of preservation of thought contents or knowledge and gave rise to the concept of library later on. The Information Technology is a blend of two words. Information means knowledge, can be bit, or a paragraph or a page.

Technology refers to the use of computer and communication technologies for gathering, processing, storage, retrieval and dissemination of information. The libraries have undergone several changes in their activities and services particularly in the areas of information storage, access and retrieval. The existence of the present information orient society is dependent on information resource; thereby librarianship is changing and expanding at a tremendous rate. Computer and communication technologies have revolutionized library and information services. Libraries are now expected to use various information technologies to provide information more expeditiously and exhaustively than before. If librarians are to play technology-oriented role, it is important that they keep abreast of the latest developments and the potential effects, which the advances in computing may have on information management. The virtual/digital libraries have brought revolutionaries changes in accessing information. The role of internet or e-learning in education and research has become multi-fold. The emergence of virtual universities has brought a dynamic change and necessitates the restructuring of syllabi. Now the Indian Universities have also started to follow this system of education. For example, the Indira Gandhi National Open University (IGNOU) has launched a number of courses on line. The Madras University has also taken initiative in this venture and offering two courses on global Information Sources and Development of Web-based courses in LIS.

Primitive Information System

The so-called information system of the primitive man consisted of sense organs as devices of receptors and conveys messages. Therefore, the transitional development in script, clay tablets, papyrus, abacus, quill pen etc. had increased the speed and accuracy in communication and information.

Categories of Resources

i. Libraries based on pre-Guttenberg technology;

ii. Libraries based on Guttenberg technology or paper based;

iii. Computerized and networked libraries; and

iv. Electronic/Digital/Virtual libraries.

4.2. SPECIAL LIBRARIES AND INFORMATION CENTRES

Special libraries and information canters are the natural outcome of the need for information support to research and development. The development of special libraries all over the world started during early 19th century. The youngest special libraries were those of technology and industry. In 1855 the Patent Office (UK) established a technological library, which is the oldest of such libraries. In India, statistics show, when the public library development was in initial stage, the special libraries of varying magnitude were growing in number steadily to meet the growing demand for information in research (Evans and Ghosh, 1959),

4.3. DIFFERENT FACETS OF INFORMATION DEVELOPMENT

Existence of CSIR

In the light of tremendous growth in the scientific and technological research after the Second World War. A major factor in this was the work of CSIR, which was founded in 1942 and now supervises 42 national research laboratories.

Creation of DRTC

During 1960s, Document Research and Training Centre (DRTC), Bangalore conducted a series of experiments to examine the feasibility of using computers in Document Finding System. DRTC developed a complete set of programs for DFS under the guidance of Prof. Neelameghan. Bhabha Atomic Research Centre (BARC) developed machine readable catalogue (MARC) of technical reports since 1970

Directory of Special Libraries

In 1962, IASLIC provided a valuable service by the publication of a Directory of Special Libraries, which give detailed information about 173 libraries, including their staff, stock, opening hours, accommodations, issue figures and finance.

Recommendations of Information Scientists, 1963.

Following the recommendations of the information scientists held in 1963, Project Oriented Central Information Service was set up on experimental basis and the first experiment took place at National Metallurgical Laboratory, Jamshedpur in 1963. The National Science Library, 1964 was developed to co-ordinate the periodical holdings of Indian scientific libraries. In 1964, INSDOC set up a small Information Retrieval Cell, which developed an alphabetization program for Union Catalogue of Scientific Serials and output was produced on punched cards (Raizada,1964)

Categorization of Indian Libraries

Indian libraries may be categorized into different generations- a large number of them without any computer application, still solely relying on manual means can be deemed as the first generation, those libraries with partial/full realization of OPAC and automated housekeeping are in the Second generation, the third generation libraries further augment their facility with multiple database access, where as libraries with full/ digital access to contents may be placed under fourth generation.

Special Libraries

A broad picture of special library scene in India has been provided by Rajgopalan (1970). His survey of 127 libraries shows that almost half of them (64) have fewer than 10,000 volumes, and most popular classification scheme is DDC (used by 50 Libraries), followed by UDC (31) libraries, followed by CC (14 libraries). During 1970, Tata Institute of Fundamental Research (TIFR) Library developed programs for generating their catalogue based on annual acquisitions (Havanur, 1975). By late 1970s, the importance of computers and on-line facility was realized and Vashishth (1979) highlighted the fact that in Western and a few other developed countries, the on-line facility had reduced the gap between the user and piece of information to zero. He suggested that effort should be made so that the Indian scientists are not at a loss. Patwardhan (1985) studied the on-line information system for providing SDI service to users at Kirloskar Electric Company Ltd. Bangalore. His study shows that SDI service offered by using on-line systems is superior both from qualitative and quantitative aspect. Krishan Kumar (1986) in his report on the conference of FID held in New Delhi, has described that there was consensus on using Facet Analysis to organize databases or knowledge bases containing highly standard and categorized knowledge. It was also emphasized that there should be collaboration between specialists in the fields of library science, computer science, linguistics, artificial intelligence, knowledge engineering and numerical taxonomy to carry out inter-disciplinary research and also to avoid duplication of research in the area of classification and communication. In 1986 an in-house database using MARC tapes for accessing documents related to computer science was developed by Murhy. Harav's (1993) review of the development of library automation in India, in last 10 years, shows that the main players in the area of library automation in 1980s have been special libraries of the country. These libraries/documentation canters are in the R&D institutions under the Council of Scientific and Industrial Research (CSIR), Indian Council of Medical Research (ICMR), Indian Council of Agricultural Research (ICAR) and the Defence Research and Development Organization (DRDO). The National Information System for Science and Technology (NISSAT) was established in 1977 with the objectives of resource development, identification of Information users and manpower development. The Environmental Information System (ENVIS), initiated by the Department of Environment, became operational in 1984.Biotechnology Information System (BTIS) was initiated in 1984 with an objective to provide variety of access mechanism to a number of international information sources on the subjects. Institution based multidisciplinary systems like INSDOC (1952) by CSIR, DESIDOC (1967) by DRDO, BARC (1954) by Department of Atomic Energy. SENDOC by the Ministry of Industries. BHEL (late 1950s) by Ministry of Industries, NML (1966) by Health Services, etc. were also set up.

Definition of Information Technology

The UNESCO has defined Information Technology (IT) as the scientific, technological and engineering disciplines and the management techniques used in information handling and processing their applications, computer and their interaction with men and machines

IT Environment in India

The Indian Statistical Institute (ISI), Kolkata was the first organization in India, which had installed HEC-2M computer system in 1955 with Russian collaboration. The ISI, Kolkata developed the first indigenous computer in 1964 in collaboration with the Jadavpur University, Kokata. On the other hand, the software industry in India is considered amongst the largest industry in the world. The National Association of Software and Service

Companies (NASSCOM) is an apex body of the software industry in India which has been effectively used towards four Es i.e., Education, Entrepreneurship, employment and Economy. The software industry has great potentiality to transform the Indian Economy and Education. The National Informatics Centre (NIC) established in 1977 is a premier I T organization in India committed to provide State-of-the-Art solutions for the I T needs of Government of India (GOI). NIC has set up a satellite based nationwide computer communication network, the NICNET, in 1988. NICNET is one of the largest VSAT based network. The Computer Maintenance Corporation (CMC) of the Department of Electronics (DoE) has installed INDONET, a commercial data network to cover entire India by setting up computer nodes at the major metropolitan cities.

IT and Its Impact

The medium of publication of Journals and other forms of literature is shifting from paper print to electronic, and their mode of distribution is also shifting. Besides, libraries have converted their card catalogues into online catalogues. Efforts are being made to provide union catalogues so that the library becomes essentially a gateway to a universe of resources in printed, electronic or other forms. Surely, all these developments are directed at creating an electronic library, a virtual library, a digital library, or a library without walls. In the information age, libraries may exist in both the states i.e. physical as well as virtual.

Use of IT in Libraries

The activities in a library mainly include the following: Collection development (Acquisition), Cataloguing and Classification, Circulation, Reference work, Preservation, Conservation and Archiving. With the availability of IT, these activities have undergone the following changes: In the selection of publications, many libraries now include paper versions but also electronic publication, including e-journals, CD-ROMs and multimedia products. Acquisition through internet has also become common. The traditional cataloguing is being replaced by on-line Public Access Catalogue (OPAC) which is a database of holdings of the library. Regarding circulation, the borrowing of journals/documents is available on internet. Reference service via internet is now available. Since library acquisitions are increasingly in non- paper forms, the preservation measures cover these media also. Besides, most of the information services like current awareness services, (CAS), Selective Dissemination Information (SDI) are computerized. Effecting quality into library and information system and services has been a continuous national and international activity of professionals. These efforts have resulted in the creation of institutional, national and international standards and specifications. The aim of education (Teaching and Learning) meant for a profession is to develop the manpower to practice that profession. Advances in IT have vastly enhanced library's capabilities of collecting, storing, processing, and transmitting information. Libraries have embraced various technologies such as computer, CDROM, telecommunications, micrographics, reprography, internet, digital libraries to enhance their efficiency and provide better and improved sources to the users. But the best thing for us would be to see that the spirit of Ranganathan's laws be made permeate the information system to ensure that the system continues to remain amenable to the needs of society.

Library Software Packages usually used in India

S. No.	*Software*	*Agency*	*Website*
01	Libsys	Libsys Coorporation	http://www.libsys.net
02	TLMS	OPAC Infosys Pvt. Ltd.	http://www.time.net
03	OASIS/ALICE	Softlnic Asia	http://www.softlinks.com

04	BASIS PLUS & TECHLIB		http://www.Idi.oc/c.ora./
05	DELSIS/ DELWINDOWS/ DOS	DELNET	http://www/delnet.ron. nic.in/
06	SUCHIKA	DESIDOC	http://www.drdo.ora./
07	SANJAY	DESSIDOC/NISSAT	http://www.nisat.org
08	MAITRAYEE	CMC India	http://www.cmc.ltd.com/
09	GRANTHALAYA	INSDOC	http://www.insdoc.org/
10	SOUL	INFLIBNET	http://www.inflibnet.org/

The success of digital project lies on sound project planning. For, study of potential clientele, study of current library services and digital resources, setting goals and objects, priorities and budget etc. In India the concept of DL is not yet full-fledged. Today the most of the research in libraries have been equipped with digital infrastructure, but there is no any kind of D Ls as developed in USA and other developed countries. In India, the internal publications like Ph.D thesis, other thesis, % 102 reports, patents, and the documents (including a few books and journals) which are not coming under copyright Act, can be digitized for subsequent access.

4.4. PRESENT TRENDS IN LIS EDUCATION & TRAINING

As per the present trend, LIS education and training be imparted in such a way so that the products rely less on collection development and more on resource sharing and networking. Similarly a lot of reflection and research will maximize the merits and minimize the demerits. Now the LIS schools have the daunting task of improving the quality and relevance of LIS education and training through improved infrastructure in the form of I T laboratories, course trained manpower, new syllabi, new approaches and methods to teaching and matching infrastructure. Library educators have to keep their doors and windows of their profession wide open making way for an inward flow of new ideas, concepts and trends emanating from neighboring disciplines. The organization has to see that its professionals continue to be productive throughout their working period. If this not taken care of, there are possibilities for the professional to become obsolete.

4.4.1. Present Scenario in Library Networking

The current status of library networking in India is that most of the libraries are covered by some network and have created databases of their holdings. The library network centers provide access either by e-mail or online or by common software. In order to have network of all Indian university libraries, the GOI under UGC established INFLIBNET (Information Library Network) at Gujarat University, Ahmedabad in 1991. The program is directed towards modernization of university libraries by introducing the installation of computers, which is basically a cooperative endeavor. The software named SOUL (Software for university libraries) was released in February, 2000. This cooperative venture for pooling, sharing and optimization of library resources, provides a channel to academicians and researchers for exchange of information from sources within the country and abroad. Library management software is being developed jointly by DESIDOC AND INFLIBNET to work under DOS and UNIX environment. Utility software for the book database on CDS/ISIS has been developed for generating catalogue cards in CDS/ISIS as per AACR-2 format from data available in ISP-2709 format having standard tags from CCF. The Indian Library Association (ILA) created a NALANDA database, under a project from National Institute of Social Science and Technology (NISSAT), which includes more than 10,000 libraries in it. NISSAT supplied CDS/ISIS packages free of charge and trained library personnel in computers led switching over to technology adoption in libraries in institutions like Bhaba Atomic Research Centre (BARC), Trombay, Central Food and

Technology Research Institute (CFTRI), Bangalore, Central Leather Research Institute (CLRI), Chennai, Bharat Heavy Engineering Limited (BHEL), Bangalore, etc.

4.4.2. Computer Application in Libraries

Computer applications in libraries may be traced to 1960's, when Indian National Scientific Documentation Centre (INSDOC), New Delhi and Documentation Research and Training Centre, (DRTC), Bangalore begin use of computers. During the year 1970's INSDOC, Publication and Information Directorate (PID, now NISCOM) of CSIR, and a few libraries in the country started automating some of their activities and services. INSDOC produced catalogue of serials using IBM/602 unit record equipment. In 1970 National Aeronautical Laboratory (NAL), Bangalore conducted experiments using ICL 1004 system for automating circulation control. By 1971, nine libraries were using computerized procedures for procurement.

4.4.3. IT Components at BLISc. and MLISc. Levels

As overview made by Chatterjee, indicates that Bachelors and Masters Programs of LIS schools reveals that very few schools incorporate IT components in the extent necessary for gaining required competencies and that too only in Masters level. Even I T get in syllabus, students do not get enough practical exposure of the modern technology due to infrastructure limitations. Moreover, due to the legacy of Dr. Ranganathan, half of the curricula is allocated to the classification of the Curriculum Development Committee (CDC) Report, 1992 under Dr. P.N. Kaula, there was some visible change in the curricula of the LIS towards the inclusion of I T components, but most of the DLIS didn't implement it.

4.4.4. Role of INFLIBNET

INFLIBNET has developed five databases- one each on books, thesis, serials, experts and research projects using CDS/ISIS (Keeping in view the west trends in I T towards middle tier architecture i.e. to provide access to middle media kits, and other accessories are absolutely inadequate in majority of the LIS departments.

4.4.5. Beginning of Online Accessing

In 1975, a one-week demonstration of online accessing of the databases held by the European Space Agency Information Retrieval system (ESA-IRS) was organized at the Tata Institute of Fundamental Research (TIFR), Bombay. In 1976, *INSDOC started Chemical Abstracts condensate and providing Selective Dissemination Information (SDI) services in the country, using the IBM 370 computer of NT Madras.

4.4.6. Practical Training

Education in any profession must respond to the needs of the profession. These changes may lead to departure from the conventional courses. It is therefore, essential for LIS schools not only to integrate the application of I T, but the practical training to students is as important as formal theoretical knowledge. It is pathetic to know that the majority of the Indian University departments are being run by either one or two full-time staff members supplemented by contributing staff, for running the courses at all levels, i.e. BLISc, MLISc and PhD programs.

4.5. INFORMATION EXPLOSION

The third quarter of the last century has witnessed immense knowledge explosion and information explosion as well. There are about three to four million articles appearing each year in some 30,OOOsignificant journals with a growth of 8-10 per cent per year. The periodical publication within just a span of 10 years has been doubling of its publication; some scientists call this as 'Information Deluge'. The advancement in IT with computer communication has made accessibility from any part of the world. In the light of these developments, most of the libraries and Information Centers (L&ICs) are flooded with modern technology.

The Rate of ALA Articles Appeared in Journals

S. No.	*Year*	*ALA Constant Number of journals*	*No. of articles produced*	*% of growth rate*
01	1980	30,000	62,000	8-10%
02	1990	30,000	1,66,000	
03	2000	30,000	40,000	

4.5.1. Need for Electronic Libraries

In 1990 Alwin Toffler in his book 'Powershift' estimated that 1.3 trillion documents are appearing only in US. By now the number must be more. Keeping in view the universe, the publication of documents will be much more. Financial constraints, budget allocation for Indian University libraries is insufficient for purchase of even 10% of books published in India. The most severe price increase occurred in reference manuals (abstracts, indexes, etc.) e.g. Chemical Abstracts rose from $12 in 1940 to $ 1450 in 1970, $ 16350 in 1994 and $ 21764 plus postal charges in 2001, which is presented in a tabular form below:

Chemical Abstract

S.No.	*Price*	*Year of Publication*
01	$12	1940
02	$1450	1970
03	$ 16350	1994
04	$21764	2001

Chemical Abstract is a journal covered globally the prominent researches in chemistry (organic and inorganic). The journals are in the abstract form, simply classified with code number. It is upgraded weekly. Millions of books in various languages on various subjects are appearing all over the world. About 2 lacks periodicals are publishing, undoubtedly majority of books and periodicals are publishing in the developed countries. Even in India more than 60,000 books in various languages are published annually. In the face of space shortage; electronic media will solve this problem to a great extent. Databases have become a universal phenomenon. DIALOG, BRC, ORBIT, INFOLINE, IRS, STN international are some of the well known online service providers using databases. Internet is the world's first digital information technology that lets anybody to send anything digital at anywhere in the world. Whereas CD-ROM is one of the largest data memories available for a commercial PC application. CD-ROM has revolutionized the complete educational world. CD-ROM offers on disc access to bibliographic database without the need of telecommunication facilities, connect time costs and communication fees. The CD-ROM system resolves many of the retrieval issues, preservation, access, storage and security of Libraries and Information Centers (L&ICs). Now most of the International journals offer some provision to access the abstracts/full-text of paper through web along with the print subscription. So the information centre is undergoing a transition from the paper-dominated manual environment to the shred access-oriented electronic environment.

4.5.2. Digital Libraries / Electronic Libraries

Digital libraries/electronic libraries are the extension of traditional libraries in the internet era. They combine the structuring and gathering of information. It is the integration of varied technologies like hardware, software, network, web, imaging or OCR, library techniques and other developing technologies for information transfer and dissemination.

4.5.3. Genesis of Virtual Library

We are experiencing disappearance of printed secondary sources of information and rely mostly on the electronic databases. Therefore, the need to up gradation and systematic automation of libraries systems in educational and research institutions is essential. The VL is formally opened its doors to the public in 1995 at Public Library of Charlotte and Mecklenburg Country (PLCMC) North Carolina. According to Lois Kilkka, a PLCMC manager—'It was the demise of the library's collection of 16 mm films and photograph records that led to the birth of the VL. The concept of VL embodies that any person who has a connection the library network (s) can access the resources of not only that library but internationally through networks like the internet, VL may have multimedia capabilities that to see graphics and listen to sound, (b) hypermedia capabilities that incorporate the techniques of hypertext and multimedia.

Definitions

1. Digital Library / Electronic library is the library where information is stored in one form (i.e. digital form) irrespective of their different forms in traditional libraries.
2. DLs/ELs are organizations that provide the resources, including the specialized staff, to select, structure, after intellectual access to, interpret, distribute, preserve the integrity of and ensure the persistence over times of collections of digital works so that they are readily and economically available for use by a definite or a set of communities.
3. Clifford Lynch (1995), redefined it as 'a system producing a community of users with coherent access to a large, organized repository of information and knowledge. The DL/EL is not just one entity, but multiple sources are seamlessly integrated'.
4. According to Berkley Digital Library Project, University of California, 1 The DL will be a collection of distributed information sources, producers of information will make it available, and consumers

will find it through the help of automated agents.'

From the above definitions, the characteristics can be briefly stated as: The DL is not a single entity, it requires technology to link the resources of many, Digital Library collections are not limited to documents surrogates, and they also include digital artifacts that cannot be represented in printed formats. The term DL/EL became popular during the last decade of the 20the Century in the advanced countries. Typically, such as DL/EL will include a number of search or navigation aids that will both operate within that particular library and allow access to other collections of information connected by networks worldwide.

Digital /Electronic /Virtual Libraries

All the three terms are being used near synonymously, which is not exactly the case. DL/EL may roughly mean one and the same thing but DL/EL may not always be networked, but would largely contain digitized information, and since a virtual library (VL) is a library without walls, spread across the globe, from where one is able to retrieve the whole world, which Sherwill describe the V L as also called EL, online library or desktop library.

Characteristics of VL (Virtual Library)

Powell defined a virtual library as ' A library with little or no physical plant of books, periodicals, reading space or support staff but one that disseminates selective information directly to distributed library customer, usually electronically. Sherwell describes characteristics of VL as :

I. There is no corresponding physical collection,

II. Documents are available in electronic format,

III. Documents are not stored in any one location,

IV. Documents can be accessed from any workstation,

V. Documents are retrieved and delivered as and when required, and

VI. Effective search and browse facilities are available.

Few Examples of Virtual Library Virtual Library

01 South Asian Virtual Library	http://www.columbia.edu/eu/libraries/indiv'area/sarai
02 India Virtual Library	http://webhead.com/wwwvl/ind ia/ind ia 2.html
03 Pakistan Virtual Library	http://www:clas.ufl.edu/users/gthursby/pak/
04 Nepal Virtual Library	http://www.catmando.com/wwwvlnD.html

Functions of VL

I. Any number of users could view one copy of document simultaneously;

II. Study material never go out of print,

III. Protects rare books,

IV. Cost- effective and cost efficient.

Creating Digital Resource

For creating a digital resource to convert print resources into digital format, adequate attention is given for selection of the material. And digitization would prevent any duplication of work and wasting of money. The library acts as an intermediary between the author and the reader. The libraries will no longer own resources, but only serve as a channel for information. The library would have to arrange the information to provide it to the user. The prospective librarians need to have primarily is a firm grounding in any of the programming languages and expertise to develop programs not only to prepare a catalogue but also to meet the demands of all sections of the library. The librarians should be able to guide the readers to right search engines. So the thrust in the syllabus has to be on the application of computers to library management and service to readers.

Infringement of Copyright

To overcome the copyright violations like, illegally photocopying, many projects are underway. ISI, now Bureau of Indian Standard, BIS is developing a system provides secure viewing through password, secure printing through encryption and water marks, guaranteed document authenticity by means of a digitally signed finger print, and use privacy. A hidden watermark in the image file of article will discourage unauthorized copying to a large extent.

4.6. IT ENVIRONMENT IN LIS SCHOOLS

The convergence of digitization, telecommunication and other devices of IT provide the LIS schools the opportunity to build an environment for learning which have implications on the core curriculum of LIS education. Students can be best prepared for technically efficient positions by introducing electronic information services on advanced IT sills and research opportunities. Even LIS schools should undertake internet based continuing education programs. Moreover, the faculty should have the state-of-the-art information technologies and relevant training on its use. They should also explore possibilities of computer based teaching for better understanding of the latest and critical concepts. Establishing IT laboratory will call for adequate infrastructure in LIS departments. Many of the problems involving in the country are rooted in lack of adequate infrastructure. Many of them do not have sufficient number of practical tools such as DDC schedules, Colon Classification schedules, classified catalogue Code and the likely. Some of the universities have started self-financing courses and the fees charged by them is in no way sufficient to met the expenditure required to be spent on maintaining technical tools laboratory and the computer laboratory, the two types of laboratories, following the impact of IT within the department.

4.6.1. Teacher Training

In the wake of more and more use of computers and IT in organization and dissemination of information through libraries, the departments of LIS are hard pressed to provide necessary education and training in this area. This can be achieved by either of the two ways: by inviting/ appointing a computer expert in the departments of LIS for delivering lecture/training the students in the use of computer training; or ii) to train existing teachers in application of computer and IT in library and information work and services and in future to appoint library science teachers with degree/diploma in computer application/ science. If the first opinion is favored, then it will be necessary to first train the computer specialists in library housekeeping jobs ana services, without which they will not be able to give the required slant to the application of IT in library work and services. It was further felt that this is much more a difficult task. Therefore, it was felt more viable to provide opportunities to existing LIS teachers for receiving training in computer application. Since they know every bit of LIS and services, they will be more amenable. As far as new recruitments in the faculty are concerned, these days the aspirants are fully equipped with required knowledge of computer application.

4.6.2. National Institute of Educational Planning and Administration (NIEPA)

National Institute of Educational Planning & Administration (NIEPA), New Delhi is an autonomous organization under the Ministry of Human Resource and Development (MHRD), Department of Secondary and Higher Education. It is an apex training institute in India for educated, planners and administrators. Its main functions cover the fields of training, research, advisory and consulting services, knowledge dissemination and networking with other institutes and international agencies.

4.7. REMODELLING LIS CURRICULUM

The UGC Subject Panel and the curriculum Development Committee (CDC) Report 2002 under the chairmanship of Prof. C.R. Karisiddapa have thoughtfully combined the traditional and modern subjects. Besides, introducing the full paper on IT Basics (Theory & Practice) and IT Applications (Theory & Practice). And IT components have been introduced in other papers as well, where ever applicable.

4.7.1. The CDC Report, 2002

The UGC Subject Panel and the CDC Report 2002 under the chairmanship of Prof.C.R. Karisiddappa have thoughtfully combined the traditional and modern subjects of studies in adequate proportion so as to enable the DLIS to choose their own structure and content of the syllabus. It was hoped that the Model Curriculum will serve as platform for change in the future. Besides introducing two full paper on I T : Basics (Theory & Practice) and I T : Applications (Theory & Practice). I T components have been introduced in other papers as well, wherever applicable. They have also emphasized upon the adoption of two years integrated course, which at one hand can ensure eliminating duplication of course content and also provide necessary time for teaching of automation and IT component and their application in library work. Imparting all these subjects in the professional would mean redefining the curriculum and teaching methodology of LIS education. Further, strengthening the LIS teaching faculty along with IT infrastructure and curriculum would in fact produce efficient information managers. The Report has also emphasized upon the adoption of two years integrated course. The CDC Report has two separate sets of curriculum. One is for two year integrated MLISc, another is for truncated BLISc and MLISc one year each. Out of seven modules for integrated course, one module is meant for IT Applications in LIS. The first unit introduces computer to LIS students along with its architecture, hardware and software; second unit introduces Operating Systems- singie version as well as multi-version- their programming language, algorithms, flow charting up to data structures; in the third unit, students are supposed to learn network architecture, fourth unit contains the basic features and tools of internet - internet services, e-mail protocols and other protocols for file transfer, transmission control, etc. unit five carries the content of Database Management System (DBMS); the sixth unit intends to teach the design and development of library house building operations and the last unit is for digital library construction and operations In the light of the current developments in the US a number of library schools have eliminated the word 'library' and call them the schools of Information Science. Similarly the librarians are called Information Brokers, Information Architects, Cyberarians, Database Consultants, Digital Librarians, Knowledge Managers, Metadata Librarians and it seems to be an ongoing process with more developments in IT. On the lines of various library schools in US, we may also think of the organization of specialized degree programs with competitive and selective enrolment to serve the needs of librarians and information specialists desiring advanced training for increase professional responsibility.

4.7.2. Need for IT Training

The role of technological change is tremendous and it is affecting all types of libraries and Information Canters (L&ICs). At the same time the library clienteles are becoming more sophisticated in their demands for information and expect librarians to respond to their needs in an efficient and up-to-date manner. The above statement shows clearly the need and necessity of proper and up to date training to the LIS professionals. If the LIS professionals are not trained in handling IT, there is a possibility of replacement of library professionals by computer professionals. And library professionals may also use their time relived from routine work for research and compilation of reference tools and will also be an important asset in the job market.

4.7.3. Agencies Imparting Training

The main sources of training in India are the library schools, INSDOC and DRTC and a few polytechnics and library associations. There is an urgent need for INSDOC & DRTC to revise and tune their apprenticeship courses to the present requirements. Moreover, being pioneering training institutes, both are to revise their training programs from time to time, so that trainees could know about the changing technological trends in LIS education & training.

INFLIBNET, NISSAT and NIC

The trio- INFLIBNET, NISSAT and NIC should conduct IT courses of one or two month's duration by charging nominal fees. This may enable large number of teachers and senior library professionals to undergo training to update them.

ILA, IATLIS & Other LIS Associations

The professional associations should create IT culture and environment among the professionals. Therefore information professionals working in libraries, they alone can merit or man our institutions. Their efficiency is our future and their inefficiency will throw into nowhere.

4.8. EDUCATION & TRAINING PROGRAMS FOR LIS PROFESSIONALS

The education and training (E & T) programs need

to be revised and restructured by the universities. The gap between the university education and training and the expertise required to handle specific expert roles especially in the use of management skill and use of computer software is largely being filled up by the professional organizations or national information centers. For instance, National Centre For Science Information (NCSI), for instance, conducts one-year training for application of information technology to library and information services.

4.8.1. Distance Education

Distance education in its chequered history of over 100 years, starting with the Chautangua continue education program initiated by the University of Chicago in the 1890s, has made use of varied technologies. Similarly, Massachusetts Institute of Technology (MIT) has announced in 2002 that it is going to put all the courses on the internet for free. For this MIT is to spend $ 100 million in 10 years. In India, the Indira Gandhi National Open University (IGNOU) New Delhi has introduced a few online courses and following suit, Madras University has also launched a few online courses. And now the infrastructure is problem, it is the universities to come forward to launch courses online so that the pressure of admission-seekers to the universities could be lessened to some extent.

4.8.2. Revival of Scientific Temper

Dr. Ramashelkar, the Director General of Council of Scientific and Industrial Research (CSIR) elected to America's Prestigious National Academy of Sciencean honor considered second best to getting a Nobel - maintains that India is well equipped to handle the research need of top NRE scientists. Apart from Tata Institute of Fundamental Research (TIFR) etc., even some universities have top class departments like the University of Hyderabad, Pune and JNU. The government recently announced a Fellowship Scheme to try and attract some of this talent. The science and technology department is offering scientists Rs. 50,000 a month, a contingency fund of Rs 5 lakh a year. It is unlikely to bring back the best. As former Union Science and Technology Minister and one of the country top scientists, Prof. MGK Menon, points out that people are in top companies and universities and many of them are at the top of their organizations. It will be difficult to match the kind of facilities and money that these people used to, like the Americans and the Brits. For instance, a professor gets about 150-200 thousand dollars a year, and teaches one or two days and work and spends the rest of the days on research and travel. For NRI scientists with strong ties to India and willing to work in India, their half time appointments seem a good way to start the process of moving back.

5

Recent Trends in Library and Information Science Education in India and Aboard

5.1. INTRODUCTION

Library and information Science education has been at cross roads from quite some time now. The profession is witnessing tremendous changes both at National as well as International levels. The LIS Education has been revolutionized by the impact of information and communication technologies (ICTS) which itself is an amalgamation of various technologies such as Barcode Technology, RFIED Technology, Computer Technology, Communications Technology, and the recent innovative

Cloud Computing technology. With the emergence of electronic and digital technologies in library environment, the profession as well as LIS Education calls for total revamp in terms of developing professional competencies, curriculum development, teaching techniques and evaluation, Accreditation and research. Library is one of the social institutions, so it is always involved in the progress and development of the society. The successful administration and organization of the Library and information canters depends upon the trained LIS professionals which is possible only through the modernization of LIS Education by preparing trained persons in the subject. Library science is a professional as well as technical subject plus a service profession. Thus the full knowledge of techniques, methods used and services provided by them is imparted through library science education to the learners and trainers.

5.2. LIBRARY AND INFORMATION SCIENCE EDUCATION (LIS) IN INDIA

The credit for starting a formal course in library education in India goes to William Alanson Bordanand Asa Don Dickinson (both students of Melvel Dewey). Bordan established a train course at the Central Library, Baroda in 1911, and Dickinson at the Punjab University, Lahore in 1915. Gradually other universities and library Associations started setting up library schools. But the library schools developed significantly only after Dr. Ranganthan became active in this area. S. R. Ranganthan was the major force in the introduction of Librarianship courses at the University of Madras (1931), Bombay University (1941), Banaras Hindu University (1941), Delhi University (1947) and many others.

5.2.1. Current Structure Levels of LIS Education

The education of librarianship is being imparted at various levels in India and has gone very drastic changes.

The main levels of LIS Education in India at present are Certificate Course, Diploma Course, Degree, Associateship in Information Science (AIS), M. Phil, PhD and D. Lit. These programs are offered on regular basis as well as through correspondence courses or distance education. Details about the levels of courses are as follows:

(a) Certificate Course : Generally certificate courses are run by library associations but some poly technique colleges, departments and affiliated colleges are also conducting these courses presently. There is no uniformity in terms of syllabus and duration of courses and are meant to trainee for semi-professional or junior level jobs after high school or senior secondary education.

(b) Undergraduate Diploma Courses : The diploma courses in LIS Education conducted at two levels, viz, undergraduate and postgraduate levels. Undergraduate courses are conducted by women polytechnics as a two year course after higher Secondary or intermediate. It prepares 1st to be junior Librarian and hold library assistant positions.

(c) Postgraduate (P. G.) Diploma Courses : Postgraduate (P. G.) courses in some selected LIS areas of specialization are offered at the University level as a one– year course after the Bachelor's of Library And Information Science program. At present, four universities and one deemed university, and a few Documentation and Research Institutes are offering these programs (Association of Indian Universities, AIU, 2007). The Universities offering these specialized Diplomas in LIS are: University of Kerala, PG Diploma in Information Technology, University of Mysore, Post MLIS Diploma in Library Automation and Networking, IGNOU, PG Diploma in Library Automation and Networking, Gandhigram Rural Institute, PG Diploma in Archives and Documentation and Management. The specialized Associateship in Documentation and Information Science is off by DRTC (Documentation Research and Training Centre, Bangalore and Associateship in Information Science by INSDOC – Indian National Scientific Documentation Centre, New Delhi, and now NISCAIR – National Institute of Science Communication and Information Resources. Also, one year training in Computer Applications in Library and information Services (Information Systems, Management and Technology) is being offered by the Indian Institute of Science, IISC, Bangalore(basically by National Centre for Science Information – NCSI). More, 2 years M. Sc course in Information Science is being offered by Birla Institute of Technology, Ranchi and M. Sc in Information Technology by the Guru Jhambeshwar University, Hissar (Haryana). IASLIC also conducts one year diploma in special Librarianship and National Archives one year dip in Archives.

(d) Bachelor of Library And Information Science (BLIS) : At present, 120 plus Universities in India are offering this Bachelor's course in LIS. The eligibility criteria for this course are graduation. There are many institutions that offer library science as an optional subject at the Bachelor's level. Also, CBSE has recently added library science course as an elective at secondary level. This Bachelors course (BLIS) in LIS is also offered through correspondence or distance mode by various universities and IGNOU is one among them. The course is recognized by UGC, as outlined in UGCs Model Curriculum 2001.

(e) Master of Library And Information Science (MLIS) : This is the Masters level course in Library and information Science. There are 99 universities and PG colleges that offer Masters Level degree course (MLIS) in India and 20 of them are offering it as two years integrated course. Majority of these universities offer one year course of BLIS (B. Lib) and followed by one year course of MLIS. The North Eastern Hill University (NEHU) was the first University to integrated MLIS course in 1986, followed by the University of Madras in 1988. Interestingly, the integrated pattern of 2 years MLIS was later recommended by the UGC under Model Curriculum in library and information Science in 2002.

(f) M.Phil. in Library and Information Science : The Research Programs in LIS at this level (M.Phil) are offered by various Universities, although majority of Universities have shifted towards PhD /integrated PhD or direct PhD in LIS in recent times. The M.Phil may be of one year or one and a half years course. The researchers have to undergo an entrance test for the admission. Completion of research program prerequisite a dissertation, course work, research publication in a journal and completion of theory papers. It was first started by Delhi University in 1978. Presently, only 15 universities in India offer M. Phil course in LIS.

(g) PhD Research Programs : This is an advanced level research program being offered after the completion of MLIS or M. Phil in the LIS. More than 39 universities in India conduct PhD research program in LIS. The basic qualification for the admission for this course is MLIS and M.Phil plus NET/SET and entrance test.

(h) D. Lit. Program : Very few universities provide the facility of D. Lit. a post-doctoral research program in LIS in India. At present only two universities namely, Banaras HinduUniversity, Varanasi and Utkal University, Bhubaneshwar run D. Lit. Research programs in LIS in India. According to the available records, only one Post-Doctoral Dr.Shukla on the topic "The work and impact of a Pioneer in library and information Science: A critical study of the works of Prithvi Nath Kaaula "has been awarded with D. Lit by Utkal University in 1998.

5.3. LIS CURRICULUM AND CURRICULUM DEVELOPMENT COMMITTEES

At the University level, after Independence, the UGC controls mainly the general course structure of various curriculums. Since inception, the UGC has given due emphasis on the curriculum design for the LIS departments along with the developments in the University and college libraries. Till now, various committees for Review of LIS curriculum have been constituted by the UGC from time to time. The recommendations made by these committees at different points of time provide valuable guidelines in respect of standardization of curriculum, enrolment, infrastructure, quality of teachers, teaching and evaluation, methodology, research programs etc. But very little has been done to implement the valuable recommendations. This is why course for BLIS is still largely of the conventional pattern except a few LIS schools where the elements of information technology have been incorporated into the curriculum. The majority of Library schools give major importance to traditional library skills like classification and cataloguing which covers almost half of the syllabus at the Bachelor's level. The Masters Degree programs are also very much traditional, although increased quantum of information, communication Technology (ICTS), information retrieval, open access technologies, management techniques and other such innovative components have been introduced. Now, the substantial efforts have taken to revise the curriculum radically to match the modern challenges and requirements of the profession. The repetition in syllabus elements between two courses has been removed to a great extends. Also, major portion of MLIS programs comprises of information communication technologies (ICTS) and other related concepts, so that LIS professionals of 21st century are well skilled and trained in handling the modern gadgets of change. Much stress is being laid on the information literacy of LIS professionals, to enable them to work effectively and efficiently in an electronic and digital library environment.

The committees to look into the various aspects of the LIS Education in the country, constituted by UGC from time to time are:

5.3.1. The Library Committee (Ranganthan Committee on Development of University and College Libraries, 1957)

To look in the various aspects of functioning and management of University and College Libraries, the UGC appointed a committee under the chairmanship of Dr Ranganthan in 1957. The final report was published in 1965 which covered all aspects of academic libraries including the education and training of professional Librarians. The committee recommended that the university departments should offer only professional courses such as BLIS, MLIS and PhD. The practice of offering certificate course by universities should be stopped and the diploma should be converted to BLIS. The committee further recommended that a university department offering only BLIS course should have a minimum of one reader, one lecturer and one demonstrator while those offering MLIS course should have at least one professor, one reader, two lecturers and two demonstrators. Moreover, a full time teacher – student ratio should not exceed 1:10 in BLIS and 1:5 in MLIS. The committee also suggested appointing a committee to look into the question of quality and standards of Library education.

5.3.2. Ranganthans Committee on library Science in Indian Universities (1965)(Review Committee on Library Science in Indian universities

UGC appointed a Review Committee in 1961 under the chairmanship of Dr Ranganthan to look into the standards of teaching and research in library science in Indian universities. The committee published its report in 1965 with a detailed review of Library science education. The committee made wide ranging recommendations on all aspects of Library education. Thesyllabus recommended by it for BLIS and MLIS was adopted with minor changes by almost all library schools in India. The practice of non-professional subjects taught by library schools like general knowledge, language, and cultural history was done away. It also suggested for re-designation of diploma in library science to BLIS and urged universities to offer only professional courses of BLIS, MLIS and PhD. The committee also urged library science departments to have a provision of six month apprenticeship before BLIS. Regarding faculty, the committee suggested a minimum of two lecturers and one reader for a department offering only BLIS course and one professor, two readers and four lecturers for a department having MLIS course also. Thus, a slight improvement over what the Library Committee (1957) had suggested. The committee report also delved on the issue of teaching strategies and evaluation and suggested at least 400 working hours during a session for BLIS. The committee emphatically called for independent teaching departments of Library Science. However, a close cooperation between the LIS department and university library was deemed essential. On research front, the committee devoted one full chapter and noticed that the research scenario was not very encouraging. The committee called upon UGC to conduct a survey of the new entrants coming out of Universities and employers to assess the need for library professionals and the quality of University products. This was the first committee which suggested the nomenclature change of the course and was readily implemented by most of the departments.

5.3.3. UGC Panel on Library and Information Science

This panel on library and information Science from Department of Library and Information Science of Delhi University while organizing two national level seminars in 1973 and 1977. The recommendations of Panel include that university departments having adequate facilities may start a two year integrated p leading to MLIS. LIS departments in the universities should have same independent status as other teaching departments. After the inclusion of the components of information Science like information storage and retrieval, computer applications etc in the LIS curriculum, the panel suggested that the nomenclature of the departments may be changed to reflect the changed curriculum. It also urged the departments with adequate infrastructure to offer research programs of M.Phil. and PhD.

5.3.4. Kaula Committee on Curriculum Development in Library and Information Science 1993

The first curriculum development committee (CDC) in LIS was appointed by the UGC under the chairmanship of Prof. P. N. Kaula in 1990. After wide ranging deliberations, the committee submitted its report in 1992. It contains, besides a well designed detailed syllabus, well thought out suggestions to LIS schools and recommendations to UGC. The committee suggested LIS schools to clearly specify the objectives of each course offered by them. Admission for the courses be on the basis of academic achievement, entrance test, and an interview. In the university courses the medium of instruction should be English. The CDC also made recommendations regarding teaching methods, aids and other infrastructural resources required for the courses. It suggested an increase over the Review Committee suggestions, in the minimum faculty strength of LIS departments. It suggested for the departments having only BLIS course one professor, one reader and three lecturers and for departments' also offering MLIS course one professor, two readers and five lecturers. It also urged the UGC to issue guidelines to all universities for treating LIS departments as science departments for allocation of equipment grants. The scheme of papers and detailed syllabus designed by the CDC remained a model for subsequent curriculum revision exercises done by the departments.

5.3.5. Karisiddapa Committee on Curriculum Development in Library and information Science (2001)

The UGC constituted the second CDC in LIS under the chairmanship of Dr. C. R. Karisiddapa in 2000, which submitted its report in 2001. It is an excellent document on curriculum containing not only syllabi and infrastructural requirements needed to be met, but also areas like allotment if marks, teaching hours and their break-up etc. It emphasized strongly for two year integrated Masters Degree course. The committee also emphasized practical component and made specific provision practice in certain papers.

The recommendations made by these committees at different points of time provide valuable guidelines in respect of standardization of curriculum, enrolment, infrastructure, quality of teachers, teaching and evaluation, methodology, research programs etc. But, unfortunately the recommendations of these committees have not been implemented in Toto. Each LIS departments has its own objectives and own organizational framework, which is particular to it. Hence, rather than functioning as some kind of master plan for curriculum, the modular structure of curriculum was suggested in an evaluative study of the first CDC report. Subsequently, the model approach and the modules incorporated in the model curriculum could be used as a basis for designing an actual curriculum. Library education has completed a century in India. During, this period, it has covered a long distance from a small beginning of short-term training to a country – wide network of Universities, colleges, polytechnics, research organizations, professional associations, etc. offering certificate, diploma, PG Diploma, Bachelor degree, Masters degree, MPHIL, PhD and even D. Lit through regular and distance modes. What is needed is consolidation and quality rather than expansion. This mushrooming of LIS Education has created a large number of half-baked unemployable youth. A broad perspective of LIS Education in the developing and developed nations like USA, UK, Australia or India gives an indication that LIS Education in India needs to enhance some of the vital aspects such as large scale integration of the allied subject fields, Harmonization of teaching – learning programs, collaboration and exchange, use of facilities offered by international and global organizations and induction of the new components are absolutely must to get recognition in the national and international job market. In view of this, it is desirable that the library the library schools of the country must adopt themselves to the changing situations, so that they can turn out better LIS professionals who can meet the challenges posed by the changing environment. Library schools that are not able to adapt themselves with the changing dynamics and aspects may become irrelevant and have to close down sooner or later in the years to come.

5.4. LIS EDUCATION AT INTERNATIONAL LEVEL

The first school in the world to provide library science education was started in USA in 1887 at Columbia College by Melvel Dewey named as "The School of Library Economy". Here the emphasis was on the library techniques and behavioural aspects of Library services in the teaching of the school. In England, the London School of Librarianship to impart library education was opened in 1912 at London. Several other library schools were founded in the USA and in the UK in the first two de of the twentieth century. By this time, there was a general feeling in the field that library education needed to be revised. This feeling lead to in an investigation requested by the Carnegie Corporation that proposed a new structure for library education based on the university system. The establishment of the graduate library school (GLS) at the University of Chicago in 1926 was one of the major results of this investigation, which according to Tortensson as a cornerstone for the foundation of a library science in a modern sense. The next major development in LIS Education came about in the 1960s when library schools started to shift the concept of study from library science to LIS (Library and Information Science, Rayward, 1997). This change reflected the gradual maturing of Library schools as academic departments that acted within a broader view of Librarianship, libraries of all kinds, archives, database, records management, retrieval-based information services.

After this period of change, the 1980s was a decade of crisis in LIS Education. At least, ten LIS programs were closed in the USA alone, including two of the most prestigious programs at the University of Chicago and at Columbia University. The ineffective leadership, isolation, conflicts with other departments such as business and computer science and the failure to promote their programs were among the factors responsible for the closings. One of the strategies used by the LIS departments in order to confront the prevailing crisis in those years was the integration of information Science into library education and by the end of the decade more than 80 percent of the LIS programs incorporated "information Science "or information in their nomenclature to reflect their expanded coverage and to help position LIS graduates for employment in the information sector. In the 1990s, LIS programs had to cope with unparalleled constant and rapid change and LIS Education at this time was fortunately responsive to the developments such as technological innovation, rapid expansion of the information economy, continued awareness of global and multicultural issues, adoption of new delivery formats, specialization and expansion in study programs and the formation of interdisciplinary partnership within and outside the University.

As per the Kaliper Advisory Committee, 2000 there are 6 major curriculum trends in LIS departments in the

USA:

i. LIS Curricula are addressing broad based information environments and problems,

ii. LIS curricula contain a unique core of courses that are user centered,

iii. LIS Schools and Programs are increasing investments and infusion on Information technology into curricula,

iv. LIS programs are experimenting with the structure of specialization of their programs,

v. LIS schools are offering instructions in different formats, and

vi. LIS schools are expanding their programs by offering degrees at multiple levels.

At the end of the 19th century and starting of the 20th century, the LIS profession in many of the towns of UK derived its educational and professional structures. This so called 'British Model' included training in the workplace in an apprenticeship mode and eventually evolved examinations in both general and specialist knowledge set by the local professional association or the Library Association (LA) of the United Kingdom. In the 2nd half of the 20th century, this model evolved into one which primarily included local training schools catering for these examinations and later first or undergraduate degrees in librarianship which was accredited by some of the LIS professional associations rather than examining bodies. These changes were in response to a variety of factors together with increasing accessibility of education, growth in the number of libraries, changes in govt. policy and by professional associations for education to support practice and promote the status of their professions. British trained librarians, working nationally and internationally favoured the concept of librarianship as a post graduate profession. It aimed as it was towards producing library leaders rather than workers. The British apprentice and undergraduate model of LIS education for librarianship influenced many Commonwealth countries for a large part of the 20th century and even in the 21st century.

5.4.1. Current Trends in LIS Education at International Level

The rapid and far-reaching developments that have occurred in the 1st two decades of the 21st century in terms of the expansion of the information economy, the development of technological innovations, the creation of vast amounts of freely available digital information and the adoption of new delivery formats have resulted in dramatic changes in the character and organization of Libraries and Information Centres throughout the world, both in the nature of the work of information professionals as well as in the ways in which users interact with the information. All this has tremendously impacted and revolutionized the whole gamut of LIS education. All these transformations have influenced and impacted the LIS education in general more dramatically in modern world in particular. Now departments and universities offering LIS education at international level operate under different names such as: School of Information Science, Computer Science and Department of Information Communication but rarely the term Library is being used in nomenclature of LIS Schools. At structural level, in UK there is an undergraduate program in Librarianship and the master's degree consists of 2 years of study. In the USA, there is no undergraduate program in librarianship rather masters degree program of one year duration. However, there is a Library Technicians' Program in the USA, which prepares students for the post of Library Assistant and other similar technical jobs.

At the curricula front, trend is towards needs of the modern information professionals. The course contents include a lot of information management techniques, and the application of computers in information handling.

There are also internship programs built-in in the curriculum. These courses equip the students to work in modern library environments with automatic systems.

With regard to teaching techniques and evaluation, apart from regular classroom lecture sessions, the library schools also organize seminars, colloquia and practical classes for computer applications relevant to Library and Information Science work. The LIS students are also encouraged to participate verbally in the class to develop their communication skills. The students are given weekly/ bi-weekly assignments on current topics to develop their understanding of the subject.

On Accreditation front, developed countries are much ahead to developing countries like India. The Institute of Information Scientists (ITS) and the Library Association (LA) conduct joint accreditation of courses since 1998 in UK. Both the accreditating bodies maintain professional register of accreditated schools. In the USA, The American Library Association established a board of education for librarianship, which developed standards for library schools in 1924 and evolved them (Rochester 2010). The committee on accreditation is now the section of The American library Association responsible for accreditating library schools.

5.5. CONFRONTING PROBLEMS OF LIS EDUCATION IN INDIA

Many challenges exist before LIS professionals to march further to meet the present and future situations and bring in quality and innovation both in teaching and practice. The ultimate aim of any course including LIS is to equip professionals with required know-how and professional capabilities which make them employable and marketable. LIS schools in India are not able to adequately respond to emerging information scenario created by the electronic publishing and dynamics of the knowledge society because of the lack of adequate faculty strength, several library schools are letting the courses go on as they are going. The course revisions, if any, are undertaken with some patches here and there, whereas the present courses are required to be completely redefined and re-casted keeping in view the contemporary information systems, global technological developments and local needs (Malhan 2011). The implications if Information and Communication Technology (ICT) and the ever growing information needs and users have transformed LIS education into a profession with a diversity of opportunities and challenges. This requires LIS professionals to make continuous value addition to services and to integrate the emerging technologies so as to cope-up with the emerging scenario. These changes are making way for a new kind of competitive work environment. There are number of problems that still persist in advancing and streamlining the LIS education. Though it is not a education field still professionals concerned with this course could not completely overcome the problems and hurdles that hinder the progress of profession now and then. The major challenges and problems affecting the up-gradation and status of the LIS education in the country are discussed below:

5.5.1. Current Structure of LIS Education

As already discussed, the LIS education for librarianship is being imparted at various levels in India form certificate course to Ph.D. research program and even D.Litt. through MLISc. and M.Phil. Courses, major LIS schools in India impart these courses under different criteria and eligibility. There is no set criterion and uniformity in enrolling the students of these levels of courses. Every individual university, college, department or poly-technique college follows its own norms and regulations. This results in different selection process, course duration, evaluation process and methodology. So, the pressing need is to revamp and restructure the current structure of LIS education in the country. The uniformity in selection process, eligibility criteria, evaluation and other rules and regulations for awarding various LIS courses should be set-in. this will enhance and improve the credibility of out-going LIS professionals and degree holders from various LIOS schools of the country.

5.5.2. Current Curriculum of LIS Schools

It has often been lamented that the current course contents of LIS programs show no relevance with the present day information demands. Most of the LIS schools in India do not impart education on modern lines and hardly come-up with the international standards. Moreover, they do not reflect the latest changes resulted by the ICT. Most of the courses are theory based. The need for restructuring the LIS curriculum has become imperative because of cut-throat competition both at institutional level as well as within the profession. Old and outdated syllabi come to no help to the professionals in the modern digital age. There is great need of restructuring old syllabus with new updated syllabus which can equip the professionals in-tune with the modern demands of the profession. Updated curriculum not only benefits professionals but help the faculties to be in touch with advanced technology.

The disparity in terms of syllabi, duration and number of papers, contents and practical moods should be made uniform. With the advent of ICT a sea change has been brought up in the study and practicality of LIS education. Due this, it has become highly important to revise and restructure the LIS curriculum. Traditional techniques and philosophical aspects prove of no use in the present day situation. More traditional components of LIS education should be supplemented with latest innovations such as Internet of Things (IoT), Information Systems, information Processing, Information Retrieval, Big Data Analytics, On-Line Publishing and others.

BLISc. course is still large of the conventional pattern except a few schools where elements of Information Technology have been introduced. The majority of library schools give major impotence to the traditional library skills like classification and cataloguing, which covers all most half of the syllabus at the Bachelor's level. The Master's Degree programs are also very much traditional, although increased quantum of ICT has been incorporated. The repetition in syllabi between the two courses needs to be removed. Revised curriculum should be capable of preparing the future professionals in order to meet the challenges enforced upon them from time to time.

5.5.3. Accreditation of LIS Schools

The purpose of accreditation of professional association/ agency is to see that course meets the professional standards of the profession, thus saving the society form poorly prepared professionals. For any field to prosper, it is essential that it fulfils the standards of education and strictly adhere to norms of it. But unfortunately in case of LIS education no national accreditation body has been framed so far in India. It is really misfortune for the profession that without fulfilling basic facilities numerous departments and colleges are being opened. It becomes the responsibility of accreditating body to ensure reasonable standards and quality output. The report of the committee on National Policy on Library and Information System has stressed the need for such an accreditating body. So far departments LIS in the universities have broadly adopted the scheme of curriculum recommended by the UGC Review Committee on library and information science in Indiana universities. Therefore it becomes natural duty of accreditation agency to see that LIS schools and departments without proper facilities and norms and regulations should not be established without its approval, and if approved at all, it should recommend minimum standards in terms of faculty strength, intake criteria, availability of teaching material, teacher-student ratio, evaluation methods, library facilities and other guidelines.

In 1976, IFLA in its annual conference passed a resolution that, "to maintain uniformity in the standards in LIS education programs in the country, the Govt. of India may be requested to create a Library Science Council on the pattern of Indian Medical Council".

5.5.4. Inadequate Competent Faculty

Adequate, competent and capable faculty forms the backbone of any profession. As the LIS curricula is becoming more flexible and choice based, LIS schools are experiencing need for specialized faculty encompassing areas such as management, ICT, behaviour science, media studies etc. The emerging trend that favours LIS schools is to employ faculty having qualifications in library and information Sciences and an additional degree in some cognate area as mentioned above. Faculty being the first pillar of excellence and there should be no compromise in recruiting and retaining competent and committed faculty. In earlier years, the UGC Review Committee (1965) rejected the practice of employing the university library staff as part-time teachers and recommended one reader and two lecturers for a department conducting BLIS program, and one professor, two readers and four lecturers for a department conducting MLIS. At present, there is acute shortage of experienced and capable faculty members in majority of developing countries like India. Authorities appoint LIS professionals with little experience on ad-hoc bases and at low salaries. There are departments that are run by a single faculty member with guest faculty from other departments and the university library. The National Knowledge Commission (NKC2006) has also recommended the establishment of a National Institute of Library And Information Science. This will enhance the learning and employability opportunities for LIS faculty.

5.5.5. Mushrooming Growth of LIS Schools

From late 20th century, the trend has been opening and establishment of numerous LIS schools in the country. Today, LIS schools are run for the sheer benefit of institution owners. These institutions and departments which In fact do not qualify for imparting certificate course, extract large fees from the students and provide no facilities for teaching – learning. Because of low-quality of LIS education from these so-called LIS schools mere production of Sub-standard and half-backed professionals fail providing opportunities to these students. There is no check and balance and no proper attention is being paid before opening /establishing any LIS school. Adequate number of Faculty members, facilities, computer laboratory and other things necessary for conducting LIS programs is not taken care of. The Mushrooming Growth of LIS Schools from every corner of the country without meeting the necessary criteria and Eligibility is rather a grave problem which is plaguing the LIS Education of the country. Also, irrational opening of LIS Schools is responsible for deterioration of LIS profession and it has become very difficult to identify the well trained and skilled professionals from half-baked ones.

5.5.6. Lack of Well Equipped Laboratory and other Facilities

Another grave problem facing LIS Education is that many LIS schools have no laboratory, library and other necessary facilities needed for practical training of LIS professionals in the modern age of information literacy. Nowadays, LIS schools are offering course on computer applications for the electronic information environment, but unfortunately departments of LIS Schools do not have facility of well equipped ICTs labs without which students do not get practical exposure. Practical training for computerized routines such as house-keeping, jobs, provision of information services, internet access, online and CD ROM searching and others is required. UGC Model Curriculum Committee (2001) has strongly recommended that apart from enriching the contents, it is necessary that LIS departments have an IT laboratory with network facilities. The laboratory so provided should be further supported with standard software packages including one or two library application software packages.

5.5.7. Teaching Techniques and Evaluation

The teaching methods at both the levels viz, Bachelors and Masters have been predominantly the lecture method. In majority of the LIS schools, the class session lasts more than four hours which translates into less time to prepare beforehand for the class. Few schools however, also have discussion sessions at the masters' level. The students are usually given monthly / bimonthly assignments to write at the master's level. Though there are some LIS schools which mandates the research project in the final semester, but their quality is always questionable. The evaluation of the students is done by continuous evaluation (assignments, session tests) and a formal examination. Sometimes there is a viva-voce before the final examination. Now the trend is towards practical work of LIS professionals than a theoretical knowledge base. So, practical skill development regarding internet, OPAC, Software Packages, Database Management System, CD-ROM Technology, Digital Library, Online Access, etc need to be stressed in the modern evaluation techniques of LIS Schools in the country. Also, a special capsule of practical training need to be provided in LIS schools whereby a LIS students are supposed to work in a library department or to get the on hand work experience of Library services and practices.

5.5.8. Apprenticeship Program

Professional courses must be provided with practicality, mere classroom theory does not help to the student to be proficient in the profession. There should be practical on hand training to handle live situations. Many schools have learnt the importance of practicality and started conducting seriously in their schools. A Memorandum of Understanding (MOU), with the libraries and information canters willing to accept the students for practical training may be signed. Such a on hand training increases the competency building of the students and give them an opportunity to learn while they work. Practicality gives more confidence and adds competency among the students to fight challenges.

5.5.9. Selection Criteria for Students

LIS Education is now becoming famous and students from all streams are opting for the field. Though, LIS is not a first choice for the students, but certainly it has attracted attention of many. So, it is important that students of good quality should be selected. Merit should not be the only criteria, but written test and interview also should be made basis for admission. There should be a standard procedure for selection of students for LIS admission.

Besides, to these broad outlined problems of the LIS Education in the country, other problems plaguing the profession from long time are lack of LIS Policy, non-uniformity in Nomenclature, Medium of Instruction, Gap between theory and practice and shortage of funds. All the LIS professionals and library Associations need to work on these problems, so that LIS profession is really uplifted and advanced in the country.

5.6. NATIONAL DIGITAL LIBRARY OF INDIA (NDL-INDIA)

Ministry of Human Resource Development (MHRD) under its National Mission on Education through Information and Communication Technology (NMEICT) has initiated the National Digital Library of India (NDL-

INDIA) pilot project to develop a framework of virtual repository of learning resources with a single window search facility in April 2015 with project cost of Rs. 39.8 crores. The National Digital Library project is coordinated by the Indian Institute of Technology, Kharagpur. The alpha version of the NDL-Phase – 1 portal has been made Operational on February 2016. Since, it is a Digital Library, it is seamlessly available without any state-wise physical or accessibility constraint. The objective is to integrate several national and international digital libraries in one single web-portal. The NDL-India provides free of cost access to its content in English and other Indian languages (10 languages). As of January 2019, NDL-India hosts 21 core plus items in its repository, with over 15 Lac volumes in English. The Library was dedicated to the nation in June 2018.Ending January 2019, it has 20 Lac users and user registration is open to users from around the world. However, contents from popular sources are only accessible to registered users. Some of these registration-only works are from sources such as:

- World eBook Library
- South Asia Archive
- OECD Library
- Satyajit Ray Society

The NDLI is accessible through mobile app. Filtered and federated searching is employed to facilitate focused searching so that learners can find out the right resource with least effort and in minimum time. NDL-India is designed to hold content of any language and provides interface support for leading Indian languages. It is being arranged to provide support of all academic levels including researchers and life-long learners, all disciplines, all popular forms of access devices and differently-abled learners. It has been developed to help students to prepare for entrance and competitive examination, to enable people to learn and prepare from best practices from all over the world and to facilitate researchers to perform inter-linked exploration from multiple sources.

In short, National Digital Library of India (NDL-India) is an all-digital library that stores information (Metadata) about different types of digital contents including books, articles, videos, audios, thesis and other educational materials relevant for users from varying educational levels and capabilities. NDL-India has been designed to benefit all kinds of users like students, teachers, researchers, librarians, library users, professionals, differently-abled users and all other life-long learners. Information can be personalized, based on the Education level, choice of language, difficulty level, media content and such other factors while other digital Libraries may not include all these choices. This is like a customized service provided in a 24*7 integrated environment to suit a user's requirement and will be like a one-stop shop for all.

5.7. NATIONAL POLICY ON LIBRARY AND INFORMATION SYSTEMS (1986)

National Policy in Library and Information Systems in our country was formulated by Raja Rammohan Roy Library Foundation (RRRLF) and Indian Library Association. The Department of Culture, Govt. of India set up a committee with Prof. D. P. Chattopadhyaya as its Chairman in October 1985 to formulate the policy at National level in library field, the final report of the committee was submitted to Government in May 1986. Thus, it came to known as Indian National Policy in Library and Information Services and Systems (1986). A policy is a statement of commitment to a generic course of action, necessary for the attainment of a goal, which here is library development. The policy is the only way to direct, manage and develop library and information systems and services in a country. Any national policy means a set of decisions taken by a National government, applying laws and regulations to orient harmonious development of information dissemination services to satisfy information needs of the nation. As, information plays very important role in the socio-economic development of the society so, sincere and vigorous efforts were thought for strengthening and upgrading of the existing systems of libraries in the country to create new facilities in the existing library system in order to be able to serve a growing demand for an increasing number of users of the libraries. For this to happen, an integrated plan for library development was needed in the country.

5.7.1. Recommendations of National Policy in Library and Information Services and Systems Committee were

- Constitution of a National Commission of Libraries to play a major role in implementing the library policy and in the progress of Library development (in 2006 National government came up with a National Knowledge Commission which again spoke about the same and in 2014, Govt. Launched National Mission For Libraries).
- Creation of an All India Library Services.
- Active involvement of the central government in public libraries development in the states.
- Public Library Development has to be supported by agencies involved in social education, rural development etc.
- University and College Libraries are to be considered academic units and their senior library staff members should be regarded as members of academic community.
- The National Library of India at Calcutta (Kolkata) should be strengthening.
- Development of a system of National libraries.

5.7.2. Features of National Policy on Library and Information Systems

The main features of National Policy on Library and Information Systems are:

1. Free Public Library system in the country.
2. Every school or college should have a library and its qualified Librarian. (As per the National Annual Status of Education Report, ASER 2018, 37% Schools are not still having proper library facilities and a Librarian).
3. Expansion of NISSAT at National, Regional, Sectorial and local levels.
4. Systems similar to NISSAT should be organized in social sciences, humanities and in languages.
5. Parental bodies should be committed to provide support and infrastructure for libraries.
6. Manpower planning and development.
7. Library Legislation and regulations for flow of information (only 21 states have till date enacted their library legislations).
8. Use of Technology.
9. Removal of Communication barriers.
10. National Network of Libraries.
11. Development of information systems and databanks in different fields.
12. National Library Board.

REFERENCES

1. Aggarwal, S. P. (1997). Library and Information Studies in India. In Library and Information Science : Parameters and Perspectives. Vol. I. Ed. By R. G. . Prashar . New Delhi, Concept. Pp 88-104.
2. Amin Saiful (2005). The Comparative Study of LIS Education in India, UK and USA.
3. Bansal, G.C.(1997). Accreditation of LIS Schools in India

and USA : A Proposal for Collaboration. In Library and Information Science :Parameters and Perspectives. Vol. I. Ed. By R. G. Prashar. New Delhi, Concept. P.245-251.

4. Daniel, Evelyn and Lazinger, Susan (1999). Guidelines for Library Information Education. IFLA Journal. Retrieved on 25 December 2018, from *http://www.ifla.org.guidlineslisedu. 1999.*

5. Karisiddappa, C. R. (2004) Library and Information Science Curriculum for Developing Countries. World Library Information Congress on 70th IFLA General Conference and Council, 22-27 August 2004. Retrieved, 10 January , 2019 from *http://www.ifla.orgvu/dg/lisdg/india/html.*

6. Krishan Kumar and Jaideep Sharma (2010). Library and information Science Education In India :A Historical Perspective. DESIDOC *Journal of Library & Information Technology. Vol. 30.No.5.pp-3-8.*

7. UNESCO (1998) A Curriculum for an Information Society. UNESCO Principal Regional Office For Asia and The Pacific, Bangkok, 1998,p 9

8. Wilson, Anthony, M. and Hermanson, Robert (1998). Education and Training Library Practitioners :A comparative study with Trends and Recommendations. *Library Trends, Vol. 46,No.3,p.467-504.* Retrieved 20 January 2019 from *http://www.librarytrends/Edu/Training/1998/html.*

6

Report of the Working Groups on Libraries

BACKGROUND

The National Knowledge Commission has been set up by the Prime Minister with the challenging mandate to transform India of the 21st century into a knowledge society. It is expected to advise the PM on matters relating to knowledge creation, knowledge dissemination and knowledge application within the diversity of the Indian scenario. The focus of the NKC is mainly the following with action oriented sub-themes:

1. Build excellence in the educational system to meet the knowledge challenges of the 21st century and increase India's competitive advantage in fields of knowledge.
2. Promote creation of knowledge in S&T, social sciences and other academic institutions.

3. Improve the management of institutions engaged in intellectual property rights.
4. Promote innovation and entrepreneurship, and knowledge applications in agriculture, industry and healthcare.
5. Promote the use of knowledge capabilities in making government an effective, transparent and accountable service provider to the citizen and promote widespread sharing of knowledge to maximize public benefit.
6. Promote the utilization of traditional knowledge.

To realize this dream which is also being called 'Mission Impossible[1]', one major all- pervading area which needs immediate and sustained attention is the Library and Information Services (LIS) sector. The stakeholders of each focus area will need well organized and systematic Library and Information Services to support these activities.

The Prime Minister, in his inaugural speech for the National Knowledge Commission on 2nd August 2005, referring specially to libraries, said "Public libraries are an extremely important element of the foundation of a knowledge economy". With these views in mind the NKC set up the Working Group on Libraries with the following broad Terms of Reference:

1. Redefine the objectives of the country's Library and Information Services (LIS) sector.
2. Identify constraints, problems and challenges relating to the LIS sector.
3. Recommend changes and reforms to address the problems and challenges relating to the LIS sector, to ensure a holistic development of information services in all areas of national activity.
4. Take necessary steps to mobilize and upgrade the existing Library and Information Systems and

Services, taking advantage of the latest advances in Information Communication Technology (ICT).

5. Explore possibilities for innovation and initiate new programs relevant to our national needs, especially to bridge the gap between the information rich and the information poor within the society.
6. Suggest means of raising standards and promoting excellence in Library and Information Science education including re-orientation and training of working professionals.
7. Assist in setting up facilities to preserve and give access to indigenous knowledge and the nation's cultural heritage.
8. Set up adequate mechanisms to monitor activities for securing the benefits of acquisition and application of knowledge for the people of India.
9. Examine any other issues that may be relevant in this context.

The Terms of Reference were the main concerns which the Working Group tried to address in its discussions. Keeping in mind the objectives of the Library and Information Science and Services (LIS) sector as laid down by the Working Group, it suggested some major areas which needed extensive discussions by professionals or experts who have specialized in different fields. Further details of the experts consulted are included in Appendix 1.

PREAMBLE

Libraries are recognized to have a social function in making knowledge publicly available to all. This role becomes even more critical in making India a knowledge society. To fulfill this potential, existing libraries must modernize their collection, services and facilities, become more pro-active and collaborate with other institutions and agencies. In today's context, libraries have to play two distinct roles - to serve as a local centre of information and knowledge, and be a local gateway to national and global knowledge. Keeping in view the above, the Mission Statement of the LIS sector should be:

The library and information sector is committed to support the creation of a knowledge society by providing equitable, high quality, cost effective access to information and knowledge resources and services to meet the informational, educational, recreational and cultural needs of the community through a range of national, institutional and public libraries.

Recognizing that the Libraries' objectives are to

- disseminate knowledge as widely as possible;
- serve as a major vehicle to facilitate creation of new knowledge;
- facilitate optimal use of knowledge by all sectors, such as government, industry, rural sector and civil society; and
- ensure that people from all sectors and all parts of the country have easy access to knowledge relevant to their needs, in their own language;

The Working Group on Libraries makes the following recommendation.

RECOMMENDATIONS

LIS Policy

1. Libraries should be included in the Concurrent List of the Constitution of India by an Act of Parliament. This will facilitate the co-ordinated development of libraries across different sectors. Though public library development is a state subject under the Constitution, the legislative framework in many states is not resilient enough to provide the required legal support and financial backing to their library sector.

2. There should eventually be a permanent National Commission on Libraries. As an interim measure, a National Mission on Libraries should be set up for a period of three years which should be converted into a permanent Commission. The Mission should be suitably empowered to cut across the usual bureaucracy in allocation of business. Further details about the National Mission on Libraries are included in Appendix2.
3. A national census of all libraries should be prepared by undertaking a nation- wide survey. A Task Force should be set up by the Department of Culture for this purpose on a priority basis. Data on the status of libraries at the national level is largely lacking, making any kind of realistic planning impossible. Collection of census data on libraries would provide baseline data for planning.
4. A survey of user needs and reading habits should be conducted at the national level as part of the National Sample Survey.
5. The LIS education and training (including in-service) should be revised and revamped. The Mission on Libraries must assess as soon as possible the manpower requirements of the country in the area of LIS management, and take necessary steps to meet the country's requirement through LIS education and training.
6. Necessary encouragement and fillip should be given to research after evaluating the research status in this field. A separate well equipped Institution for Advanced Training and Research in Library and Information Science and Services should be set up. For further details, see Appendix3.

Finance

1. A specified percentage of the Central and State education budgets must be ear-marked for libraries.

In addition, a Central Library Fund should be instituted to take care of upgrading existing libraries over a period of 3-5years. In the first estimate, the total value of this fund may be Rs. 1,000 crores. This fund should be administered by an empowered national committee appointed by the National Mission/ Commission on Libraries.

Library Management

1. Appropriate steps must be taken by all institutions/ organizations that run their own libraries to ensure that they meet the four objectives of the LIS sector stated above in the Preamble. The Government of India should issue a notification to all institutions/ organizations to take appropriate steps to ensure that libraries working under their aegis meet these objectives. Individual libraries should be asked to display them as a library charter. A sample charter is enclosed as Appendix 4.
2. To fulfill its role in the present and changing context, each library must have a well-rounded collection relevant to its user community. A specific percentage of the budget should be earmarked for this purpose in every institution. The collection may be supplemented by access to networks and e-resources to achieve qualitative and quantitative standards (further guidelines in this regard are given in Appendix5).
3. The basic expectations from libraries of all types (public, academic, national, and special)include:
   - identifying potential users
   - analyzing users' needs
   - developing services for groups and individuals
   - introducing customer-care policies
   - promoting user education
   - cooperating and sharing resources

- developing electronic network-based services
- ensuring access to services
- Providing inviting, attractive and functional library buildings and premises.

To provide access to knowledge and resources, each library must provide a range of services to meet the needs of a diverse user community (further details are given in Appendix 6).

4. All libraries in India must have the following facilities:

   I. Trained and adequate staff - motivated, courteous and helpful

   II. Easy access and user-friendly retrieval systems

   III. Appropriate furniture, stacking and display facilities

   IV. Effective signage

   V. Computers with internet access, scanners, photocopiers, etc.

   VI. Pleasant, aesthetic and functional ambience

   VII. Facilities such as drinking water, cafeteria (for larger libraries) and clean toilets

5. Each library should monitor and evaluate its collection and services on a regular basis. All libraries should collect and maintain data on various activities and submit the data periodically to a central evaluation agency, eg RRRLF for public libraries. (See Appendix7.)

6. It is necessary to involve different stakeholders, including civil society and user groups, in the managerial decision-making process of libraries. Public libraries must be run by local self-government through committees of civil society representing users of the library.

7. Services for special groups need to be provided through assistive technologies; for example, The

National, State and District libraries should develop special collections and services for the visually challenged and hearing impaired.

8. Recognizing the role of reference service in meeting the information needs of individuals, efforts must be made at the national level to provide a good reference service. Libraries with experience, necessary tools and subject expertise could come together to set up a centralized collaborative virtual enquiry handling system using the latest Information Communication Technology (ICT).

9. Recognizing that there are other centers of knowledge in a geographical area and that there is a need to capture knowledge about the local community, be it a village or a town, libraries need to expand their role to include community information. Libraries should integrate with all other knowledge-based activities in the local area to develop a community-based information system. It is expected that Libraries will be involved in creation and dissemination of area-specific content and relevant information. In the rural sector, each village library would play a critical role. The responsibility for this must lie with the Panchayats. Community Knowledge Centers should be set up in close proximity or on the premises of schools. Integrated development of all information-generating agencies such as government departments, NGOs, etc is of critical importance for this purpose. In town/ metropolitan areas, enabling services such as lists of visitors, public lectures, local history, etc should be provided for the various institutions in the area.

10. To optimize resources, efforts should be made to synergize the strengths of different types of libraries, eg a school library may serve as the children's section of the public library.

Access and Networking

A critical aspect of Library services is proper and easy access to all types of resources. It is essential that standardized collection organization techniques are followed.

1. To permit local, national and global access, catalogues of all libraries should be computerized and put on a website in a format that will allow search of any bibliographic record across the libraries.
2. Networking of Public Libraries should be undertaken in a phased manner, and completed within a period of five years.
3. A National Repository of Bibliographic Records should be set up with downloading and uploading facilities which will evolve into a National Union Catalogue. A separate Committee, headed by an expert of high public and professional credibility, should be set up for this purpose. For further details on Points XVIII - XX, refer to Appendix 8.
4. The software needs of the LIS sector may be specified and the capabilities and ingenuity of civil society may be utilized for preparing such software. Suitable incentives may be offered for the same.

Private Collections

1. A National Committee on Private Collections should be set up for identification, documentation and preservation of the numerous rich private collections available in the country. The Committee may be set up under the Chairpersonship of an eminent scholar. The Terms of Reference are enclosed in Appendix9.
2. Since special facilities for maintaining private collections are not easily available, it is suggested that Ten Regional Centers be set up by the Government of India in different parts of India to

house selected and approved private collections. These centers should be located in Delhi, Kolkata, Guwahati, Pune, Bangalore, Hyderabad, Chennai, Ahmedabad, Patna and Jammu.

Digitization and Open Access

To enable equitable and universal access to knowledge resources, it is important to create more digital resources which can be shared. The concept of an "information commons" i.e. "resources shared by a community of producers and consumers in an open access environment"[3] needs to be promoted. New resources should be openly accessible and historical documents, too, should be digitized and made available. *www.parliament.vic.gov.au/sarc/E-democracy/Final_Report/Glossary.html*

1. This Working Group strongly recommends that peer-reviewed published research papers resulting from publicly funded research in India must be made available through open access channels, subject to copyright regulations. The group also recommends use of open standards and free and open source software.
2. All pre-independence periodicals and newspapers in all Indian languages and in English must be digitized for access and preservation. To help preserve digital resources, optimize their use and avoid duplication of effort:
3. State-level archives for preservation of digitized materials must be setup.
4. Every State should establish a registry and archives of knowledge-based digital resources, and make it accessible.

Staffing Pattern

1. In the changed context, it is necessary to assess the

manpower requirements for different types of libraries and departments of library and information science, keeping in mind job descriptions, qualifications, designations, pay scale, career advancement, service conditions, etc. Further details are included in Appendix10.

Public Private Partnerships

1. Philanthropic organizations and other private agencies should be encouraged to support existing libraries set up by the government or set up new libraries. These organizations may provide financial support, technical and professional expertise, equipment and infrastructure.

APPENDICES

1

The following are the Members of the Working Group:

1. Smt. Kalpana Dasgupta (Chairperson)
   Former Director, Central Secretariat Library, New Delhi
2. Dr. S. Arunachalam
   Distinguished Fellow, M.S. Swaminathan Research Foundation, Chennai
3. Mr. K.K.Banerjee
   Director, Raja Rammohan Roy Library Foundation, Kolkata
4. Mr. K. Jayakumar
   Joint Secretary, Ministry of Culture, New Delhi
5. Dr. H.K. Kaul
   Founding Director, DELNET, New Delhi
6. Mr. K.K.Kochukoshy
   Librarian, Central Reference Library, Kolkata
7. Mr. Manoj Kumar K.
   Acting Director, INFLIBNET, Ahmedabad
8. Prof. S. Mandal
   Director, National Library, Kolkata
9. Prof. P.B. Mangla
   Former Head of Dept. of Library and Information Science, University of Delhi
10. Dr. T.A.V.Murthy
    Librarian, CIEFL, Hyderabad
11. Dr. Harsha Parekh
    Former Head of Dept. of Library Science and University Librarian, SNDT Women's University, Mumbai

12. Dr. A.R.D.Prasad
    Associate Professor, Documentation Research and Training Centre, Indian Statistical Institute, Bangalore

The following Committees were set up with specialists and professionals experienced in the stated areas of activity:

1. Committee on Database Creation and Networking

Smt. Kalpana Dasgupta (Chairperson)
Former Director, Central Secretariat Library, New Delhi

Mr. K.K. Banerjee
Director, Raja Rammohan Roy Library Foundation, Kolkata

Dr. H.K. Kaul
Founding Director, DELNET, New Delhi

Mr. K.K. Kochukoshy
Librarian, Central Reference Library, Kolkata

Mr. Manoj Kumar K.
Acting Director, INFLIBNET, Ahmedabad

Dr. T.A.V. Murthy
Librarian, CIEFL, Hyderabad

Dr. A.R.D. Prasad
Associate Professor, Documentation Research and Training Centre, Indian Statistical Institute, Bangalore

2. Committee on Private Collections

Smt. Kalpana Dasgupta (Chairperson)
Former Director, Central Secretariat Library, New Delhi

Dr. Imtiaz Ahmad
Director, Khuda Baksh Oriental Public Library, Patna

Dr. Ramesh Gaur
Librarian, IGNCA, New Delhi

Dr. Arun Ghosh
Former Librarian, Centre for Social Studies, ICSSR, Kolkata

Dr. Sudha Gopalakrishnan
Mission Director, National Mission for Manuscripts, IGNCA, New Delhi

Dr. H.K. Kaul
Founding Director, DELNET, New Delhi

Dr. T.A.V. Murthy
Librarian, CIEFL, Hyderabad

Dr. Usha Thakkar
Honorary Secretary, Mani Bhavan Gandhi Sangrahalya, Mumbai

3. Committee to set standards and modalities for collection development, systems and services

Smt. Kalpana Dasgupta (Chairperson)
Former Director, Central Secretariat Library, New Delhi

Dr. Jagdish Arora
Chief Librarian, IIT Delhi

Mr. Frank Christopher
Joint Director, Parliament Library, New Delhi

Dr. P.R. Goswami
Director, National Social Science Documentation Centre, New Delhi

Mr. P. Jayarajan
Former Head, British Council Libraries

Mr. K.K. Kochukoshy
Librarian, Central Reference Library, Kolkata

Dr. Harsha Parekh
Former Head of Dept. of Library Science and University Librarian, SNDT Women's University, Mumbai

4. Committee on Staffing Pattern and Staff requirement of Libraries

Smt. Kalpana Dasgupta (Chairperson)
Former Director, Central Secretariat Library, New Delhi

Mr. K.K. Banerjee
Director, Raja Rammohan Roy Library Foundation, Kolkata

Dr. S.M. Dhawan
Former Scientist F and Head, Library and Information Services, National Physical Laboratory, New Delhi

Dr. S. Majumdar
University Librarian, Central Reference Library, Delhi University

Prof. S. Mandal
Director, National Library, Kolkata

Prof. P.B. Mangla
Former Head of Dept. of Library and Information Science, University of Delhi

Mr. E. Rama Reddy
Former Librarian, University of Hyderabad

Meeting dates and venues

- The Working Group met on 17th April, 27th May, 13-14th July and 14th August, 2006.
- The Committee on Database Creation and Networking met on 17th May and 23rd June, 2006.
- The Committee on Private Collections met on 19th May and 26th June, 2006.
- The Committee to set standards and modalities for collection development, systems and services met on 22nd May and 28th June, 2006.
- The Committee on Staffing Pattern and staff requirements of libraries met on 15th May and 30th June, 2006.

All the above meetings were held at the Centre for Cellular and Molecular Biology, Hyderabad; the Centre for Policy Research, New Delhi; and the National Library, Kolkata.

The Vice Chairman of the NKC, Prof. P.M. Bhargava attended all the Working Group meetings and made significant contribution to their deliberations. Shriya Anand and Chandana Chakrabarti were present at all the meetings of the Working Group and ably supported the deliberations of the Working Group and the Committee meetings.

2

National Mission on Library and Information Services (NMLIS)

Library and information services are fundamental to the goals of creating, disseminating, optimally utilizing and preserving knowledge. They are instrumental in transforming an unequal, traditional society into an egalitarian, progressive knowledge society. Developments in information communication technology (ICT) have enabled libraries to provide access to one and all, and also bridge the gap between the local, the national and the global.

Yet the Library and Information Services (LIS) sector in India has not developed, by and large, to keep pace with the paradigmatic changes taking place in society. It is imperative that all libraries (public, academic, research and special) change gear and develop at an accelerated pace. At present, being a State subject and coming under the purview of different apex agencies, there is no common direction or coordination among them.

The National Knowledge Commission with its focus on knowledge creation, knowledge application and knowledge dissemination, has rightly addressed the problems and prospects of the LIS sector. To give a proper direction to the sector which has so far developed in a very haphazard way, there is a felt need to set up a body which will deal with this sector in a more rational manner. The activities which are now being performed as piecemeal and isolated ventures by different agencies may be streamlined for the benefit of a much larger group of stakeholders at all levels. A National Mission on LIS must be set up for a period of three years with statutory backing and a regular budget.

The Role of the NMLIS

1. Advise the government on Libraries and Information Sector
2. Set standards for collection, services and technical processing
3. Encourage public/ private participation
4. Interact with State Governments
5. Conserve cultural heritage
6. Review and assess LIS education & In-service training needs
7. Support R&D/ technological development
8. Ensure access to all publications including government and institutional public documents

The NMLIS should be converted into a permanent National Commission on LIS in not more than three years, to become an important part of the development process.

NMLIS and later the National Commission should be headed by a person of eminence and high public credibility with demonstrated interest in and knowledge of libraries.

3

Indian Institute of Library and Information Science (ILIS)

India has a long tradition of libraries and has contributed to the development of basic concepts in the discipline such as fundamental principles of library services and knowledge organization tools. However, R&D activities in LIS today are extremely limited. Library and Information Services (LIS), though concerned with global information resources, need to pay close attention to the local environment. The diversities within the country in terms of socio-economic-cultural factors, the multiplicity of languages, varying levels of literacy and educational achievements and access to information and communication technologies, make it essential that planning for LIS take into account the ground realities. Further, the exponential rate of change and innovation relating to this discipline also warrants intensive R& D initiatives. It is also necessary to provide guidelines and training for implementation of tools and technology so that research results are effectively utilized.

Much of the research in the field of LIS is being adopted and utilized in organizing the Internet. It is generally accepted that the present search engines lack semantic knowledge of the documents processed. Whether it is a huge collection of information within a Library or Internet, the tools and techniques that have long been used by Library and Information Science professionals will be of immense help in making the Web a "Semantic web". Especially Prof. Ranganathan's major contribution in the area of classification has evolved as Web Ontology.

His faceted classification system has had a clear influence on exchangeable Faceted Metadata Language (XFML). In addition to classification, another major area of Library and Information Science i.e. cataloguing (metadata) also has had a great impact on the organization of Internet documents. Many standards like Dublin Core, Metadata Encoding and Transmission Standard (METS) are being evolved. Another major area that is gaining importance is the concept of Digital Libraries, wherein scientists and researchers can make their publications accessible to their fellow researchers.

Keeping the above in view, it is felt that a national institute for advanced training and R&D in LIS needs to be set up. The proposed Institute would have two major functions:

a. To offer training programs in relevant areas and to conduct continuing education programs (including training of trainers) for the library and information professionals

b. To identify, sponsor and conduct R&D programs in the field of Library and Information Science, including newly emerging research areas. Among the areas needing immediate R&D, the following were identified by the Working Group

   - User needs for different groups
   - Reading habits
   - Organization of community information and development of appropriate standards
   - Standardization of Indian names
   - Vocabulary control over Indian subjects developed in terms of multi- lingual thesauri and subject heading lists
   - Development of open source software
   - Development of Digital Libraries, both in English and Indian languages

- Technical standards for Indian scripts, Optical Character Recognition (OCR) for Indian scripts, and search engines which can implement stemming algorithms for Indian languages.
- Cross Language Information Retrieval with an emphasis on information in Indian Languages

The Institute's scientists will basically concentrate and carry out research in major areas contributing to Libraries and Information Science. In addition, they can undertake externally funded projects and provide consultancy to other organizations.

The Institute will also undertake activities to disseminate the research findings such as printed and online publications, seminars and conferences, web portal, etc.

Proposed Organizational Structure

Advisory Board

Director (Administrative Head)
Research groups for different activities
other supporting staff

Aegis

The Institute (suggested name: Indian Institute of Library and Information Science) would logically function under Ministry of Culture as major libraries of India including The National Library are already under its purview.

4

To seek commitment from all institutions/ organizations that run their own libraries, towards the four objectives of the LIS sector stated in the preamble, it is suggested that each library evolve its own charter of services. An example is given below:

The Library Charter

Recognizing that the objectives of the library are to:

- Disseminate knowledge as widely as possible.
- Serve as a major vehicle to facilitate creation of new knowledge.
- Facilitate optimal use of knowledge by all sectors, such as government, industry, rural sector and civil society.
- Ensure that people from all sectors and all parts of the country have easy access to knowledge relevant to their needs, in their own language.

The Library Understands to

- Serve as the local centre of information and a gateway to national and global knowledge providing fair access to knowledge and information to as many users as possible
- Offer an inviting and attractive physical space with clean drinking water and toilet facilities
- Offer proactive services to its user communities
- Ensure that users are treated with courtesy and respect by library staff
- Pay attention to the needs of children, women senior citizens and the physically challenged
- Optimize its potential to provide access to information and knowledge to all

- Help users develop information skills to make optimum use of resources
- Improve its collections and services on a continuing basis in consultation with users
- To work more effectively and efficiently by undertaking every activity in a professional manner
- To bridge the gap between the information poor and the information rich

5

Identification of types of materials

It is recognized that the types of materials available in different libraries are varied, depending on the size and special features of individual libraries (see Table 1).

QUALITATIVE AND QUANTITATIVE GUIDELINES FOR COLLECTION DEVELOPMENT

General Guidelines

1. All libraries must maintain a well-rounded core collection, including reference material to satisfy the regular needs of its user community. These may be supplemented through networks, e-resources, etc, to achieve better qualitative and quantitative standards.
2. Library collections are dynamic resources and there should be, therefore, constant renewal of materials to ensure that the collection remains relevant to the user communities.
3. Except in the case of national repositories, weeding out should be a regular process. Each library should evolve a weeding out policy, approved by the competent authority.
4. The criteria for categorizing libraries in government and public libraries and grading of librarians should be reviewed keeping in mind factors such as size of collection, immediacy index[4], users, services and access to electronic resources.

Public library collections

1. The size and nature of the collection should reflect the population and local requirements.
2. Locally relevant language material should be available.
3. Book purchase should be a continuous process and at least 10% of the book collection should be less than five years old.
4. At least 60% of the library's budget should be spent on collection development.

Academic Library Collections

1. In general, the library collection of academic institutions should take into account the number of disciplines offered, the level of the courses, the number of students and faculty and the research activities of the parent organization.
2. At least 6 – 10% of the total institutional budget should be utilized for collection development on a recurring basis.
3. For a new college / university or a course, a one-time budget may be provided for setting up the basic collection.

Special Library Collections

1. In the case of special libraries, the collection should be relevant to the specific research needs and thrusts of the institution. Further, depending on their areas of interest, they should acquire materials at the national and international research fronts of their disciplines. The library should acquire books and journals to meet at least 80% of the internal requirements of its user community.

National Library Collections

1. In the case of the National Library and other national

level libraries, the collections should be as comprehensive as possible.

Table 1. Types of materials generally available in different types of libraries

Type of Library	*Public*	*School*	*Academic*	*Special*	*National*
BOOKS					
General books	✓	✓	✓	✓	✓
Reference books	✓	✓	✓	✓	✓
Textbooks	✓	✓	✓		
Rare books			✓	✓	✓
PERIODICALS					
Magazines	✓	✓	✓	✓	✓
Academic journals			✓	✓	✓
Newspapers	✓	✓	✓	✓	✓
GREY LITERATURE					
Reports			✓	✓	✓
Theses			✓	✓	✓
Institutional publications			✓	✓	✓
Conference papers			✓	✓	✓
Official documents			✓	✓	✓
AV MATERIAL (in all media)					
Audio	✓	✓			
Video	✓	✓			
Photographs	To be available in all libraries, depending				
Films	on relevance				
Microfilms			✓	✓	✓
Multimedia	✓	✓	✓	✓	✓
E-RESOURCES (offline/online)					
Databases –Bibliographic			✓	✓	✓
Full-text databases (including e-journalsand e-books)			✓	✓	✓
Locally digitized materials	✓		✓	✓	✓
ARCHIVED MATERIAL					
Manuscripts			✓	✓	✓
Personal papers (correspondence/diaries)			✓	✓	✓

Government records		✓	✓
Oral history		✓	✓
Community Information	✓		
Traditional Knowledge		✓	

6

Kinds of Services to Provided by the Libraries

1. Kinds of services to be provided by all libraries[5]:

(i) Lending of materials for home use : however this will not apply to special libraries or special collections in libraries. The National Library should distinguish between its statutory functions as a national repository and its historical obligations as a public library. In course of time it should develop ways and means of segregating these functions.

(ii) Reading facilities on premises – need to be attractive, bright and comfortable. Opening hours should be at the convenience of readers. Libraries should be closed only on national holidays.

(iii) Reference service : Providing qualified and willing staff (knowledge workers) for acting as intermediaries between the users and the collection

(iv) Providing Internet access to link the local library to national and global information

The above four basic services should be free to users at point of use.

The following services may be made available

(against payment wherever appropriate), depending on the size of the library and the needs of the user community.

1. Inter-library loan
2. Photocopying
3. Document delivery, including Electronic Document Delivery(EDD)
4. Extension services in public and academic libraries for women, children, senior citizens and physically challenged persons
5. Community information services
6. OPAC (Online Public Access Catalogue)
7. Electronic/AV resources, workstations and appropriate infrastructure for use and delivery
8. Training users in information literacy
9. Institutional repositories of research articles, reports, institutional publications and Electronic Theses and Dissertations(ETD)
10. Websites, portals, subject gateways, etc (especially in case of special libraries)
11. Digitization of rare resources (before any digitization program, one must consider what is to be digitized and whether any other libraries have undertaken similar exercises)
12. Identify non-users and promote the use of libraries among them.
13. A periodical review to determine the needs of users and effectiveness of services should be conducted by libraries.

2. Consortia of libraries/ institutions with a common membership should be instituted, facilitated and encouraged.

3. Besides offering routine library services, libraries should initiate new and imaginative services in consultation with the local community, such as:

- Discussion centering around books
- Lectures and discussions on subjects that affect the local citizens
- Cultural programs to showcase local talents
- Celebration of important events and occasions
- Support to students' homework and projects
- Help to prepare for competitive examinations
- Introducing young children to books and reading
- IT training at different levels

4. All academic institutions must set up institutional repositories of ETD. This should be made mandatory for accreditation. Such repositories should be made open access.

5. All public academic and research institutes should be encouraged to set up freely accessible institutional repositories of their full-text articles and publications subject to copyright restrictions.

Table 2. Services to be provided in different types of libraries

Type of Library	*Public*	*School*	*Academic*	*Special*	*National*
Lending of materials for home use	✓	✓	✓	✓	
Reading facilities on premises	✓	✓	✓	✓	✓
Reference: qualified staff	✓	✓	✓	✓	✓
Internet access	✓	✓	✓	✓	✓
Inter-library loans	✓		✓	✓	
Photocopying	✓	✓	✓	✓	✓
Document delivery (incl. EDD)*			✓	✓	✓
Extension services for women, children, etc.	✓	✓	✓		
Community Information Services	✓	✓			
OPAC	✓	✓	✓	✓	✓
Electronic/ AV resources, workstations	✓		✓	✓	✓

Training users in information literacy	✓	✓	✓		
Institutional repositories			✓	✓	
Websites, portals, subject gateways, etc.			✓	✓	✓
Digitization of rare resources			✓	✓	✓
Identification of non-users	✓	✓	✓	✓	✓

7

Collection of Statistical Data

Statistics should be collected on the following and be used for monitoring and evaluation:

1. Percentage of registered users' to population.
2. Percentage of collection on loan on any given day.
3. Number of books lent during a stated period.
4. Average books issued per user per unit time.
5. Number of books (including journals, documents, etc.) consulted in house per member per unit time.
6. Number of reference queries answered per unit time.
7. Number of registered users.
8. Number of recommendations received for purchase of books per year.
9. Number of library publications produced by the library per year.
10. Number of books withdrawn from collection per year.
11. Number of photocopies made per unit time.
12. Number of hours that the reading room is open per week.

8

Access Mechanism

The key to opening the resources of a library is its access mechanism. In today's context it is possible to use technology to bring together the resources of small individual libraries into one seamless large library. The ability to retrieve information from this library depends on standardization of classification, cataloguing, database structuring and exchange formats.

1. COLLECTION ORGANIZATION AND INTEGRATED ACCESS

Local access

i. Access to every document (print and electronic) in a library should be possible through a proper system of cataloguing and classification.

ii. To help all libraries accomplish this task easily and without delay, and to ensure optimal utilization of expertise and resources, it is essential to develop bibliographic utilities which permit downloading of records (catalogue entries) and uploading of holdings information by all libraries.

iii. Libraries having collections of print and electronic resources should provide integrated access using latest ICT.

National and Global Access

i. Union catalogues (print and electronic) of learned periodicals should be updated and put online.

ii. Projects should be developed by the National Library and the Central Reference Library, with support of institutions such as National Book Trust, Sahitya Akademi, Central Institute of Indian Languages at Mysore, C-DAC, and Departments of Library and Information Science in order to:

   a. Convert Indian language scripts/ dialects to Roman script.

   b. Develop convenient Authority Files for rendering of names of Indian authors and institutions.

iii. Vocabulary control over Indian subjects should be developed in terms of multi-lingual thesauri and subject heading lists.

2. INFRASTRUCTURE REQUIREMENTS FOR CATALOGUING, DATABASE CREATION AND NETWORKING

(a) Open source software should be used wherever possible at present and eventually at all levels.

(b) An open source web-enabled library management software should be developed if necessary and provided to all public libraries for facilitating networking. This software should support multiple Indian language scripts/dialects.

3. NETWORKING OF PUBLIC LIBRARIES

(a) Networking of public libraries should be undertaken in a phased manner. There are approximately 54,000 public libraries in existence; they should be networked in a phased manner.

- 1,000 of these will be networked in Phase I as a pilot project, by DELNET and INFLIBNET, each covering about 500 libraries in 12 – 18 months.
- Phase II: Based on the experiences of Phase I, up to 10,000 libraries will be covered in one year.

- Phase III: The remaining libraries may be networked in the third and final phase in three years.

This project should be completed by 2011.

(b) RRRLF may give the necessary infrastructural support for the above activity and co-ordinate it.

(c) The networking agencies should ensure state-of-the-art technology with the following features:

i. Open source platform for the software, which also supports multi- lingual environment with multi-user and multimedia content creation capabilities.

ii. Storage, dissemination and replication of the data through mirror sites, gateways, portals, and inter-library loan facilities.

iii. Capabilities of conducting exhaustive training programs.

4. NATIONAL REPOSITORY OF BIBLIOGRAPHIC RECORDS

(a) The central repository will contain records of bibliographic resources available in the country.

(b) State central libraries and district / municipal / sub-divisional libraries should be provided with a server with dedicated internet connectivity, and should be responsible for creating bibliographic records.

(c) The libraries at block / village level should have broadband connectivity to enable them not only to access internet but also to create and upload local content to the library next in hierarchy.

(d) For this purpose, the present infrastructural facilities provided by agencies such as BSNL, MTNL, or other ISPs, should be used.

(e) A separate Committee, headed by an expert of high public and professional credibility, should be set up for this purpose. The Terms of Reference of this Committee should be as follows:

Terms of Reference for the Committee on National Repository of Bibliographic Records

1. To define the scope and objectives of the proposed National Repository of Bibliographic Records.
2. To take stock of the existing situation with regard to bibliographic records.
3. To suggest technical and operational details and necessary linkages to achieve the above.
4. To assess the strengths and weaknesses of the stakeholders in effectively participating in this program
5. To evaluate the adequacy of the existing legal framework for this purpose and suggest suitable measure.
6. To critically evaluate the capabilities of National Library and Central Reference Library as designated agencies for creation of the National Bibliographic Repository and suggest suitable measures for strengthening them.

9

National Committee on Private Collection

Recognizing the importance of private and personal collections in the knowledge creation and dissemination process, and the fact that there are several rich and valuable private and personal collections in existence in the country which need to be preserved for posterity, there should be an effort to include them in the Library and Information Service Sector. For this purpose, a National Committee should be set up under the Chairpersonship of an eminent scholar. The Total of Rs and other details for implementation may be as follows:

Terms of Reference for National Committee on Private Collections

1. To survey and assess the national situation with regard to identification, documentation and preservation of private collections.
   (a) Identification of existing collections in the country.
   (b) Identification of nodal repositories across the country.
   (c) To carry out a survey at two levels–
      - a survey at a national and state level to identify the existing institutions and private/ personal collections, and

- a survey of private and institutional collections at the micro-level.

(d) The survey should be undertaken keeping in mind the following guidelines: *Categorization of private collections* (heritage and contemporary)

Type of Collections

1. Personal and private collections of historical and cultural value
2. Institutional collections

Type of Materials

1. Manuscripts
2. Old and rare printed materials and historical documents
3. Letters and diaries
4. Contemporary documents of historical and cultural relevance
5. Audio visual material
6. Other materials such as awards, medals, citations, etc.

2. To suggest a decentralization model for identifying, documenting and preserving private collections and creating an institutional network at the national and state level.

3. To develop institutional networks to make available inventories or catalogues of private collections, with a view to disseminate information regarding the availability of these collections as well as to create wareness.

4. To evolve effective measures and schemes for conservation and preservation, documentation and sharing of information on private collections.

(a) *Conservation and Preservation*

i. A directory of conservation and preservation experts and institutions should be compiled.

ii. Survey and documentation of existing methodologies of preservation, both indigenous and international, should be carried out and kept updated to include new state-of-the-art technologies.

iii. New technologies for preservation should be introduced at all levels.

iv. Standards and benchmarks for conservation of different materials should be prepared.

v. Archives for digital documents should be established in each State/Union Territory.

(b) *Documentation*

i. Descriptive cataloguing of personal and private collections should be introduced.

ii. International standards should be maintained in the cataloguing.

iii. Nodal agencies at the state and national level may be entrusted with the responsibility of conducting the surveys mentioned earlier, and cataloguing the private collections. Necessary financial support should be extended to these agencies.

(c) *Dissemination*

i. The catalogues of private collections created at the national and state level should be accessible through the web.

ii. Private records and collections of importance should be digitized into full text form with proper indexing facilities and should be made available to users against payment where appropriate.

iii. Archives of digital documents should also be made accessible through the web.

5. To outline suitable advocacy and outreach strategies for this purpose.

(a) Sensitize individuals and institutions / business houses about the value and significance of private collections as national property, cultural heritage and historical sources.

(b) Use audio-visual and electronic media for creating greater awareness about such collections among different sections of society.

(c) Have information about private collections reach all levels of society including administrators, scholars, students and the general public.

(d) Have extension activities organized through different media, by the concerned institutions, to generate awareness about the merits, use and importance of private collections.

6. To formulate necessary approaches for human resource development and creation of infrastructure.

Human Resource

(a) A system of training may be established in areas such as cataloguing, conservation and preservation, digitization, digital archiving, archival management, rare languages and scripts.

(b) Existing institutions which have the capacity to undertake the management, digitization, documentation, etc, of private collections, should be suitably supported for this purpose.

Infrastructure

(a) Existing nodal agencies and their network of associated institutions should be provided suitable infrastructural facilities such as computers, printers, internet access, multilingual software, manpower, in accordance with certain minimum standards laid down by the Committee.

7. To evaluate the adequacy of existing policy and legal framework and suggest suitable measures to ensure that:

   (a) Valuable personal collections are not destroyed or sold/ smuggled out of India.

   (b) Everyone has a right to access the contents of those private and personal collections that are supported by the government, except those excluded by mutual agreement.

   (c) Owners of private and personal collections provide access to their collections by:

   - Voluntary permission
   - Access/ use fee
   - On the basis of mutually agreed terms

   (d) Institutions supported by government that maintain archival materials be strengthened to archive documents and disseminate these materials for use to the public. The institutions must create a user-friendly environment for providing this access. Access guidelines should be formulated and made available to the users. Enabling legal provisions for access need to be formulated with the help of legal experts, and made available to all concerned.

8. To develop guidelines for owners of private collections:

   The National Committee may formulate the detailed guidelines, keeping in view the following:

   (a) Copyright issues and the application of Right to Information Act

(b) Proprietary rights

(c) Government support for individuals having private collections, especially for conservation and publication

(d) Training facilities for individuals having private collections

(e) Terms and conditions for the acquisition, donation or loan of private collections

(f) Terms of reference under which collections could be digitized for wider dissemination

(g) Any other issue emanating from local situations.

10

Staffing Pattern and Staff Requirement of Libraries

Libraries should be classified into the following –

i. National Library and other national level subject libraries

ii. Public Libraries (Public Libraries may follow a four/five tier system.)

iii. Academic Libraries (academic library system will be a three tier system comprising university, college and school libraries)

iv. Special Libraries including Government Libraries (special libraries would comprise R&D libraries, industrial libraries, and specialized libraries)

Skills required to fulfill this changing role –

i. Library and information handling skills.

ii. ICT knowledge skills.

iii. Communication and training skills.

iv. Marketing and presentation skills.

v. Understanding of cultural diversity.

vi. Knowledge mapping skills.

STAFFING PATTERN AND STAFF REQUIREMENT OF VARIOUS TYPES OF LIBRARIES

I. National Library

The National Library, Kolkata has been categorized as Category VI Library in the OM dated 24 July 1990. National Library is the only library in India which has been mentioned in the Constitution of India as an Institution of national importance. Therefore, it must be developed into an institute of excellence of high academic standing.

The Department of Culture may review the staffing pattern of the National Library and the Central Reference Library in context of their changing roles and national responsibilities.

II. Public Libraries

a. As regards the nomenclature of different levels, it was felt that the libraries may be categorized as follows

   i. State Central Library

   ii. District Library

   iii. Sub-divisional/ Town Library

   iv. Rural Knowledge Centre/ Community Information Centre

b. To ensure that the services match the changing scenario, these libraries will also act as Knowledge Centres[6] and be expected to perform the

   Each of these libraries will be networked within the present hierarchical structure of public libraries. Following types of activities in addition to the library's routine responsibilities (the lists given below are only indicative and not exhaustive):

   (i) State Central Library : Information service, e-learning, knowledge management, knowledge centre activities, content creation and management, subject gateways, content analysis, collaborative publishing, e-governance, training.

   (ii) District Library : Information service, e-governance, content development, co-ordination of rural knowledge centers.

   (iii) Sub-divisional/ Town Library : Lending of

books, reference services, inter-library loan, web-based services such as e-learning, banking and insurance, community information, content and database creation.

(iv) Rural Knowledge Centre/ Community Information Centre : Lending of books, web-based services such as e-learning, banking and insurance, panchayat-level information, e-governance, community information, content and database creation.

c. There should be proper co-ordination of activities between the different levels of Libraries, especially in respect of those activities which will be of common interest, e.g. training, sharing of databases and contents, problem solving, transaction analysis, gathering of information towards developing uniform standards and modeling of inspection of need, access and dissemination, and inspection of progress of knowledge based activities and identifying weaknesses in the system, if any.

d. Keeping in view the above categorization, the following staff structure is recommended.

   i. Managerial (Group A)

   ii. Professional/ Technical Staff (Group B)

   iii. Para-professional/ Support Staff (Group C)

e. The Head of the Library at each level may be designated as State Librarian, District Librarian and Town Librarian. It is also suggested that the following routine jobs may be outsourced: Stack management, library binding, stock verification, retro conversion, bar coding, borrowers' registration, digitization, library security and upkeep, physical infrastructure and maintenance, computer network and maintenance. Work of administrative staff such as Night Watchman, Cleaner, Mali, Driver, Book Binder and Sweeper may also be outsourced.

State Central Library (Category III Library)

I. Managerial Staff (Group A)
   - i. State Librarian
   - ii. Deputy Library Director
   - iii. Assistant Library Director (presently designated as Information Officer)

II. Professional/ Technical Staff (Group B)
   - i. Information Assistant
   - ii. Junior Information Assistant
   - iii. Data Entry Operator

III. Para-professional/ Support Staff (Group C)
   - i. Library Attendant

IV. Administrative Staff
   - i. Administrative Officer
   - ii. Stenographer
   - iii. Cashier
   - iv. Administrative Support Staff
   - vi. Night Watchman, Cleaner, Mali, Driver, Book Binder, Sweeper, etc, to be outsourced

District Library (Category II Library)

I. Managerial Staff (Group A)
   - i. District Librarian

II. Professional/ Technical Staff (Group B)
   - i. Information Assistant
   - ii. Data Entry Operator

III. Para-professional/ Support Staff (Group C)
   - i. Library Attendant

IV. Administrative Staff
   - i. Night Watchman, Cleaner, Mali, Driver, Book Binder, Sweeper, etc, to be outsourced

Sub-divisional/ Town Library (Category I Library)

I. Managerial Staff (Group A)

   i. Town Librarian

II. Professional/ Technical Staff (Group B)

   i. Data Entry Operator

III. Para-professional/ Support Staff (Group C)

   i. Library Attendant

IV. Administrative Staff

   i. Night Watchman, Cleaner, Mali, Book Binder, Sweeper, etc, to be outsourced

Rural Knowledge Centre/Community Information Centre (Block Level)

I. Professional/ Technical Staff (Group B)

   i. Information Assistant

II. Para-professional/ Support Staff (Group C)

   i. Library Attendant

III. Administrative Staff

   i. Village Level Volunteers

f. An Information Officer is needed to look after and co-ordinate the activities of clusters of four to six District Libraries and their Knowledge Centers.

III. Academic Libraries

a. The academic library system comprises of the following types of Libraries:

   i. School Libraries
      - Primary Schools
      - Secondary Schools
      - Higher Secondary Schools

   ii. College Libraries
      - Junior Colleges
      - Degree Colleges

- P.G. Colleges

iii. University Libraries

b. Keeping in view the changing scenario and the new responsibilities, the existing staffing pattern, duties and qualifications should be reviewed and altered wherever required to meet the new challenges. The existing designations may also be reviewed by the NMLIS/ National Commission.

IV. Special and Government Libraries

Special libraries are parts of parent institutions and, unlike public and academic libraries, do not enjoy any individual identity in their staffing structure. In the emerging knowledge society era, special libraries must be reshaped as knowledge management centers that will require linking people, knowledge, and technology that would facilitate knowledge flow and transfer to foster knowledge assimilation and knowledge creation.

Staffing Pattern

The situation may be assessed keeping in mind the new functions and services expected in the present changing scenario. Since special libraries are the part of parent institutions, their staffing pattern has to conform to the staffing pattern of the organizations of which they are part. Therefore the group recommended as follows:

- Special libraries should have the same staffing pattern and also the same promotional avenues as are available to other staff in the same organization.
- The Library staff in special libraries and information centers must be treated at par with the staff of the same level in the parent organization in terms of class of post, qualification, pay scale, service conditions and career advancement.
- A new staffing formula for special libraries needs to be evolved to enable them to serve more effectively.

- Government Libraries

Categorization of government libraries should be in accordance with the OM dated 24 July 1990, which was issued on the basis of the recommendations of the Review Committee on Library Staff, under the purview of the Central Government 1988, which were accepted by the IVth and Vth Pay Commissions.

Keeping in view the changing scenario and new responsibilities, the staffing pattern, duties and qualifications may be changed wherever necessary. The designations may be reviewed and new suitable designations may be suggested in the government sector.

V. Staffing Pattern of LIS Departments

a. A system should be set up to foster close co-operation between the teaching/ research faculty and practicing librarians at all academic and research institutions, by measures such as–

   i. Mobility of staff (in terms of recruitment and in terms of teaching) should be made possible.

   ii. Practicing librarians and experts should be associated with the teaching faculty for offering specialized courses.

   iii. Similarly, teachers could be associated with libraries as consultants, for carrying out projects, and for carrying out continuing education programs to practicing librarians, etc.

b. The minimum staffing pattern for the BLISc. course should be as follows:

   i. Professor 1

   ii. Reader 1

   iii. Lecturers 2

c. The minimum staffing pattern for the MLISc. course should be as follows:

   i. Professor 1

ii. Readers 2

iii. Lecturers 4

d. There should be a 1:10 student teacher ratio.

e. It was felt that the Department should have not more than 50 students in one class for BLISc. course, 20 students for MLISc. course, and Ph.D. students according to the University norms.

f. All departments of LIS should set up computer laboratories and well- equipped departmental libraries with appropriate teaching tools.

g. Appropriate physical facilities such as classrooms, must be made available to each LIS department.

h. E-learning materials for upgrading the skills of the existing staff should be provided.

i. Teachers who will teach in areas such as ICT applications in libraries and other modern methods, should have specialized in these areas. A system must be set up to allow stringent review of the performance of teachers. A suitable system of rewards, including promotion, should be instituted.

Jobs to be done in Libraries

Keeping in mind the regular and specialized activities of different types of libraries, there are mainly four categories of staff in libraries at present–

- Non-professional (Category1)
- Semi-professional (Category2)
- Professional (Category3)
- Managerial (Category4)

In **Category 1**, posts such as Library Attendants, dusting bearers, etc are generally expected to perform routine duties for instance, dusting and cleaning operations, pasting and labeling on books, arranging books and periodicals, preparing sets for binding, etc. The upkeep of the library is their main responsibility.

Category 2 comprises designations such as Library Assistants, Junior Professional Assistants, etc. These staff members deal with the actual library operations such as data entry, purchase orders and book supply, manning the circulation desk, maintenance of membership records, physical stock verification, etc.

Category 3 includes professional assistants and assistant librarians. The Professional Assistants are the backbone of all professional activities of any library. They are involved in all activities pertaining to acquisition of books and periodicals; cataloguing and classification of books and other documents, maintenance of the OPAC, reference services, circulation and lending services.

The Assistant Librarians work as sectional heads and supervise all the professional and non-professional activities of the division(s) under their supervision. The assistant librarians are also responsible for planning new activities and preparing the budget proposals as and when required.

Category 4 includes the Librarian/ Head of the library and Deputy Librarian (or equivalent).

Deputy Librarian

The Deputy Librarians are primarily engaged as Heads of Divisions and involved in handling and supervising day to day services, activities as personnel management, coordination between sections/ divisions, user services, reference services, cataloging and classification and public relations, computerization, digitization and IT applications. They assist the Librarian/ Head of the Library in all matters and also provide efficient Library services.

Librarian/ Head of the Library

The following are the fundamental and common duties expected to be performed by the Librarian/ Head of the Library:

1. To formulate and administer policies, rules, and regulations for the purpose of making the best possible use of the Library by the community
2. To interface with the different stake holders, including decision making authorities and user communities
3. To plan, organize and implement modern management methods including ICT applications to provide improved library services.
4. Overall responsibility of Library functioning and supporting the informational/ educational/ recreational/ cultural needs of the user communities at all levels.

The above list is only illustrative and not exhaustive. With the development of new technologies, this list may change. Allocation of jobs may be made by the library authority according to the needs of the library. However, the culture of the library should be such that no one should refuse to do any job which the person can perform since the operation of the library should be a collective responsibility.